*To Julie Tillman---
high school graduate, a sweet
girl looking to the sky for
an exciting career!*

A Living
Sacrifice

Fourth in the *Wise Woman* Series

by
Bessie Patterson

*Love Always,
Bessie Patterson*

QUALITY PUBLICATIONS
P.O. BOX 1060
ABILENE, TEXAS 79604
(915) 677-6262

ISBN: 0-89137-436-1

Dedication

To our three daughters—Gerry Bennett, Nancy Ward, and Sherry Coldwell—with love and appreciation for all we have been able to share with them and their families . . . and to each woman who offers her life as a living sacrifice to the glory of God and our Savior, Jesus Christ.

Credits

Table of Contents

Prologue

This book is presented as the fourth in a series of five "Wise Woman" books. However, each of the four may be considered and used as an independent study for you as an individual or in a Bible class for women. My prayer is simply that it be used to stimulate your study of God's Word and its application in your life.

We will be studying primarily in the Book of Romans, with special emphasis on the 12th chapter. We will be discussing Christian attitudes and duties motivated by God's grace in response to our need.

Again, I emphasize that we are not studying **about** the Bible—we are studying **the Bible**! You are encouraged to deepen your knowledge by doing your own research on the topics considered in each lesson. To enrich each class period—or your own study of each chapter—daily Bible readings are being suggested.

Also included with each lesson are suggested memory passages. Moses said to the children of Israel, "These words which I command you this day shall be upon your heart" (Deuteronomy 6:6). Remember when you said, "I know that **by heart**?" You meant that you knew it word for word. Nothing in the world, when stored in your mind, can be more profitable than the word of God. It may not be easy for you to memorize, but you **can** do it. Write the passage being studied on a file card and keep it handy. Try! Heed the frequent admonitions to "give diligence." "Make every effort" to know and do God's will:

> *Make every effort to supplement your faith with virtue, and virtue with knowledge, and knowledge with self-control, and self-control with steadfastness, and steadfastness with godliness, and godliness with brotherly affection, and brotherly affection with love . . . Wherefore the rather, brethren, give diligence to make your calling and election sure: for if ye do these things, ye shall never fall: For so an*

entrance shall be ministered unto you abundantly into the
everlasting kingdom of our Lord and Saviour Jesus Christ.

—2 Peter 5b-7, RSV; 10,11, KJ

Your diligence will be rewarded with comfort, counsel, and growth!

I am not inspired as the New Testament writers were, but I **am** inspired by what they wrote. The deep study necessary for this type of effort is rewarding and humbling. We never can exhaust the riches of God's Word! Please be aware that many of the words in this book **are inspired** because they are quoted directly from the Bible. Again, I have compared various translations and chosen those which seemed most helpful in the thought being considered. This study is in no way to be a commentary on the scriptures. Rather, I am attempting to let the Bible speak through me. Any comments I make are to be used simply to encourage you to apply biblical thoughts to your own life.

I must again disclaim complete originality in thought and comment. Many teachers, preachers, and lecturers have contributed to my spiritual growth, so ideas from many sources will be included, consciously or unconsciously. Where possible, credit will be given, but I express my sincere gratitude to God and to all who have shared in the enrichment of my spiritual life. As you use this material and other books I have been privileged to write, please feel free to call on me for further help in your own growth toward spiritual maturity.

Above all, I want to express my own dependence on the Lord, on Jesus Christ as the head of the church of which I am privileged to be a member, and on the power available to each of us through the ministry of the Holy Spirit. I thank God for His marvelous gifts! I exclaim with Paul:

Oh the depth of the riches of the wisdom and knowledge of God!
How unsearchable his judgments, and his paths beyond tracing out!
Who has known the mind of the Lord?
Or who has been his counselor?
Who has ever given to God, that God should repay him?
For from him and through him and to him are all things.
To him be the glory forever! Amen.

—Romans 11:33-36 NIV

In Christian love,

Bessie (Mrs. Elmer) Patterson

Chapter 1

From Darkness to Light

Introduction: "Therefore, I urge you, brothers, in view of God's mercy, to offer your bodies as living sacrifices, holy and pleasing to God—which is your spiritual worship." This was Paul's urgent plea to the Roman Christians—a plea I am accepting as I am asking you to do. We may ask, "But **why**, Paul?" Why **should** I be a living sacrifice?

Note the **therefore** in Romans 12:1, quoted above from the NIV. It is a powerful little word, here used as an adverb modifying, or explaining the phrase, "to offer your bodies as living sacrifices." **Because** of things discussed in the previous chapters of Romans, Paul is making a strong appeal: "I **urge, beg, beseech** you." Let's do an overview of those first 11 chapters to motivate us to respond to the apostle's urgent plea. We hope to accomplish this goal in our first three lessons.

    I. There is a hint of the light to come in Paul's salutation and prayer opening Chapter 1. He identifies himself as the bearer of "Good News"—the gospel, of which he is a messenger unashamed. In Verse 16, he identifies the news he is presenting as God's **power** to save all people, Jews and Gentiles alike. **But** something is standing between us and that power! Beginning in Verse 18, the author paints a dark picture identifying that which makes God angry, thus cutting off His power to us, as **sin**.

        A. As much as we loathe dwelling on the negative, we must understand what sin is from God's viewpoint; we must understand what sin can do to our lives.

            1. All unrighteousness is sin according to Paul in Verse 29, King James; other translations say "all kinds of wrong," "all manner of wickedness," "rottenness" and "with every kind of injustice, mischief, rapacity."

Paul spells out so clearly that none can misunderstand the heinous character of sin:

People knew God. But they did not give glory to God and they did not thank him. People's thinking became useless. Their foolish minds were filled with darkness (sin). People said they were wise, and they became fools. People gave up the glory of God who lives forever. People traded that glory for the worship of idols . . . People were full of sin, wanting only to do evil things. So God left them and let them go their sinful way. And so they became full of sexual sins, using their bodies wrongly with each other. Those people traded the truth of God for a lie . . . People did not think it was important to have a true knowledge of God . . . Those people are filled with every kind of sin, evil, selfishness, and hatred. Those people are full of jealousy, murder, fighting, lying, and thinking the worst things about each other. Those people gossip and say evil things about each other. Those people hate God. They are rude and conceited and boast about themselves. Those people invent ways of doing evil. They don't obey their parents, they are foolish, they don't keep their promises, and they show no kindness or mercy to other people. Those people know God's law. They know that God's law says that people who live like this should die. But they continue to do these wrong things. And they also feel that people who do these things are doing right (Romans 1:21-23a; 24,25a; 28a; 29-32, ERV).

2. Later in his epistle, Paul declares one is condemned if his action does not spring from faith: "But he who has doubts is condemned, if he eats, because he does not act from faith; for whatever does not proceed from faith is sin" (Romans 14:23, RSV).

3. John says simply, "Sin is the transgression of the law" (1 John 3:4b, KJ). The Simple English Bible says plainly, "Sin is breaking God's law." Of course, you know what it means to transgress, to step over the line. Maybe you heard your brothers say, after drawing a line on the ground, "Just step over that line, and we'll fight." God's laws are as plain as that mark on the ground, and if we break them deliberately, we must suffer the consequences. That makes God angry (Romans 1:18).

4. Then there are sins of omission. Someone has said these are sins we forgot to commit. Hardly! Remember when you forgot to make up your bed before going to school? That was a transgression of your parents' law; you were guilty of failure to do what you knew you should do. James puts it this way: "A person sins when he knows he should do something good but doesn't do it" (James 4:17, SEB).

Certainly telling a friend or neighbor about Jesus is something good. But do I fail to do so because I am afraid of offending them? Am I afraid

10

that showing them from the scriptures that they are lost because they have obeyed the commandments of men rather than the word of God will upset them (Matthew 15:9)?

Meeting with others for Bible study and worship is surely good. Are you sinning when you neglect such opportunities for some trivial excuse rather than a valid reason, such as illness or being providentially hindered (Hebrews 10:25)?

We are told to love our children, our husbands, our neighbors, our brothers and sisters in Christ—even our enemies. Those things are good. Neglecting to do them is sin. Sharing our material possessions—even a cup of cold water—is good. If I neglect to do so, am I to be classified among the vile sinners pointed out by Paul in Romans 1? (See Titus 2:4; Mark 12:31; Romans 13:10; 1 Peter 1:22; Matthew 5:44; Romans 12:20; James 2:15-18; Mark 9:41.)

B. But how could a nice person like you sin? You may be deceived; sin is deceptive! After quoting the command "Thou shalt not covet" in his powerful picture of the struggle between the spirit and the flesh, Paul says, "For sin, finding opportunity in the commandment, deceived me and by it killed me" (Romans 7:11, RSV). To the Ephesians he admonishes, "You were taught to put away your old way of living. It will destroy you. Those evil desires can fool you" (Ephesians 4:22, SEB). Because others are doing it—perhaps even those we love and respect—we can be lulled into thinking evil is good.

C. Sin is separation from God. All accountable persons who have not obeyed the gospel are separated from God because of sin (2 Thessalonians 1:8). Even Christians can sin and thus be separated from God. In writing to the Corinthians Paul said, "The person who thinks he is safe should be careful—he might fall!" (1 Corinthians 10:12, SEB). The prophet Isaiah had warned, "But your iniquities have separated between you and your God, and your sins have hid his face from you, that he will not hear" (Isaiah 59:2, KJ).

D. Sin is destructive. Physical and spiritual death came about because of sin. We read, "Sin came into the world through one man. And death came into the world through sin. In this way, death spread to all men, because all sinned" (Romans 5:12, SEB). We might assume that only physical death is implied here, but that spiritual death results from sin is made clear: "For the wages of sin is death" (Romans 6:23a).

E. Sin is universal. This is one time the common excuse "Everybody's doing it" is correct. Certainly, not everyone is doing each of the catalogued sins, but each of us at some time does something that separates from God, even if it is just neglecting to obey the gospel. We might be living an exemplary life, but if we refuse to accept the

11

sacrifice Jesus made for us, the good life we live on our own counts for nothing. In fact, we insult God if we say we have not sinned. "If we say we have not sinned, we make him a liar, and his word is not in us" (1 John 1:10, RSV).

A prophetic statement from Isaiah recognized the universality of sin and foretold that Christ would bear all our sins to the cross: "All we like sheep have gone astray; we have turned every one to his own way; and the Lord hath laid on him the iniquity of us all" (Isaiah 53:6, KJ).

II. It was necessary for Paul, in writing to the Gentile Romans, to show them that they were included in God's plan for the salvation through Jesus Christ. The Jews had been God's people for a purpose, but Jesus fulfilled that purpose. Therefore, all nations—every person, you and I—are as subject to the **universal salvation** as we were to universal sin. Paul turns eloquently to scriptures recorded in the Old Testament to clinch this point:

What should we say? Are Jews better off: Not at all! We have already proved that all Jews and also non-Jews are under sin's POWER. This is written:

"No one is good—not even one person! No one understands. No one is looking for God. All men have turned away from God and become completely useless. No one is kind—not even one person!" (Psalm 14:1-3; Ecclesiastes 7:20).

"Their throats are like an open grave. They use their tongues to trick people" (Psalm 5:9).

"Like dangerous snakes, poison is under their lips" (Psalm 140:3).

"Their mouths are filled with cursing and bitterness" (Psalm 10:7).

"They move quickly to kill someone. After they leave, people are suffering and destroyed. They have not known the peaceful way" (Isaiah 59:7-8).

"They do not fear God" (Psalm 36:1).

*Now without the law, the way God makes people right has been revealed. The law and the prophets point toward this truth. Committing oneself to Jesus Christ is what makes a person right with God. **Salvation** is for anyone who **believes**! It makes no difference who you are, because everyone has sinned and is far away from God's glory. But with God's gracious love, we are made right with God through Christ Jesus who sets us free" (Romans 3:9-24, SEB).*

A. Just as universal sin is dependent on the individual's response to God's will, universal salvation is not a blanket covering everyone, regardless of his attitude of heart. God is the judge; his judgment is righteous. Perhaps you have heard someone say, "I cannot believe that a loving God would condemn a person to eternal punishment." By inspiration, Paul answers that question, too:

> Will you escape God's condemnation? Do you look down on God's kindness, tolerance, and patience? Surely you know that God's kindness is meant to lead you to a change of heart.
>
> But your heart is hard and unchanged. You are storing up punishment for yourself on the Day of punishment when God's righteous judgment will be revealed. God will pay back each person according to the way that person lived. Eternal life will go to those who, by patiently doing good things, are looking for glory, honor, and life with no end. But punishment and anger will go to those who are following wrong, by being selfish and not obeying truth. There will be trouble and pain for every human being who does evil. This is true, first for a Jew, then also for a non-Jew. God treats everyone alike . . . On that Day, God will use this Good News of mine to judge the secret things of men through Jesus Christ (Romans 2:3b-11,16, SEB).

B. How will God judge? Notice he will use the Good News, or **gospel** as rendered by other translators. We will appear before the judgment seat of God just as those who are accused of breaking the law appear before the court of their district, where a judge appointed or elected to hear each case will sit.

In a general sense, we think of the gospel as including the teachings of Christ; it is confirmed by Jesus Himself that all will be judged by what He said: "He who rejects me and does not receive my sayings has a judge; the word that I have spoken will be his judge on the last day" (John 12:48, RSV). He continued by saying that He had not spoken on His own authority but according to what God had told Him to say.

Just as God chose to communicate with us through Jesus, the living Word (Hebrews 1:1; John 1:1,14), He also delegated the judging of all people to the Christ. In his sermon to the first Gentile converts at the house of Cornelius, Peter concluded with Jesus as the righteous judge: "Jesus commanded us to preach to the people. He told us to tell them that he is the one whom God chose to be the judge of all people, living or dead. Every person who commits himself to Jesus will be forgiven through the authority of Jesus. All of the prophets say that this is true . . ." (Acts 10:42,43, SEB).

13

III. If we had been left with Paul's picture of the darkness of sin, causing God's anger, we would be unable to grope our way out of our guilt. But the inspired writer points us to Jesus, who is described by John as the light: "In him was life, and the life was the light of men. The light shines in the darkness, and the darkness has not overcome it" (John 1:4,5, RSV).

Thus, God's grace is revealed to us. He sent His son so that we who were lost in sin might be saved through our faith in Jesus Christ. "Grace" usually is defined as "unmerited favor"; certainly, by nothing that we could do would we deserve such a loving gift. One translation uses **gracious love** where others use **grace**: "But where sin increased, God's gracious love overflowed much more. Sin used death to rule. In the same way, God's gracious love rules through righteousness through our Lord Jesus Christ for eternal life" (Romans 5:20b,21, SEB).

A. We remain in the darkness of sin unless we believe that Jesus Christ **is** God's son. Actually, our faith in Jesus gives us access to God's grace, in which we find peace: "Therefore being justified by faith, we have peace with God through our Lord Jesus Christ: By whom we have access by faith into this grace wherein we stand, and rejoice in hope of the glory of God" (Romans 5:1,2, KJ).

Jesus said, "I have come as light into the world, that whoever believes in me may not remain in darkness" (John 12:46, RSV).

B. From the above passages, we might conclude that faith alone—simply believing in Jesus as the Son of God—equals salvation. We will go into the means of our appropriation of salvation through Christ more thoroughly in our next lesson. We would not dwell on this subject, but some reputed scholars have propounded, and many have based their hope of salvation on, the doctrine of faith only. Just as we cannot be saved while dead in sin, we cannot be saved by faith which is dead:

> *My brothers, if a person claims he has faith, but he will not serve God, what good is that kind of faith? Can a "faith" like that save him? Suppose a brother or sister needs clothing or daily food. And you say, "Go in peace. I hope you will find enough clothes to keep you warm and will have plenty to eat!" Unless you give them what they need, what good have you done? So even faith is dead, when it is alone and will not act (James 2:14-17, SEB).*

Bible students have pointed out that the only place in the Bible where we see the term **faith only** is in James 2:24: "Ye see then how that by works a man is justified, and not by faith only" (KJ). In the same chapter, James uses faithful Abraham as an example of faith and action, or work, working together, concluding, "His faith was made perfect by the things he did." The writer of Hebrews elaborates on Abraham's willingness to obey God's command to offer Isaac, the son of promise, as a sacrifice. His faith was so strong that he was willing to obey, trusting that God could fulfill His promise in Isaac even by raising him from the dead (Hebrews 11:17,18).

C. To appreciate fully the salvation from the devastation of sin in our own lives, we must realize that Jesus Christ, the sinless one, assumed our burden of sin, carrying it with Him to the cross. Isaiah had drawn a graphic picture of the Savior's assuming our guilt:

> *Surely he hath borne our griefs, and carried our sorrows: yet we did esteem him stricken, smitten of God, and afflicted. But he was wounded for our transgressions, he was bruised for our iniquities: the chastisement of our peace was upon him; and with his stripes we are healed. All we like sheep have gone astray; we have turned every one to his own way; and the Lord hath laid on him the iniquity of us all (Isaiah 53:4-6, KJ).*

Our sinless Savior came to save the world, to destroy sin: "You know that he appeared to take away sins, and in him there is no sin" (1 John 3:5, RSV). Jesus, our high priest, through whom we may be presented sinless before God, was tempted in every point as we are, but without sinning (Hebrews 4:15). Paul made the cost of Christ's atoning quite plain: "God was reconciling the world to himself in Christ, not counting men's sins against them . . . God made him who had no sin to be sin for us, so that in him we might become the righteousness of God" (2 Corinthians 5:19,21, NIV).

D. You may become the **righteousness of God?** I am sure you must feel as I do. That I might be so blessed almost takes my breath away. **How** can I be worthy of such tremendous love expressed in Christ's sacrifice for me? All He really asks is that I divest myself of **self** reliance and realize my total dependence on God. In the sermon on the mount Jesus said, "Blessed are the poor in spirit, for theirs is the kingdom of heaven" (Matthew 5:3, KJ). But how do I translate being "poor in spirit" into my life? Does that mean I am to be namby-pamby, having no direction, without spirit? Not at all! But it does mean that I cannot achieve God's righteousness alone. One of the newer translations may make this concept more workable in our lives: "Those people who **know they** have great spiritual needs are blessed. The kingdom of heaven belongs to those people" (Matthew 5:3, ERV).

Conclusion: In view of God's sending Christ to become sin for you, surely now you are ready to plead as David did:

Have mercy on me, O God, according to your unfailing love; according to your great compassion blot out my transgressions. Wash away all my iniquity and cleanse me from my sin. For I know my transgressions, and my sin is always before me. Against you, you only, have I sinned and done what is evil in your sight, so that you are proved right when you speak and justified when you judge (Psalm 51:1-4, NIV).

Daily Bible Reading

Sunday
The Gospel— God's Power
(Romans 1:1-17)

Monday
Sin's Dark Picture
(Romans 1:21-32)

Tuesday
Recognizing Sin
(Romans 14:23; 1 John 3:4; James 4:17;
Romans 7:11; Ephesians 4:22; Isaiah 59:2)

Wednesday
Sin Universal
(Romans 5:1-19)

Thursday
Universal Salvation in Christ
(Romans 3:9-26)

Friday
Condemnation or Glory
(Romans 2:1-16)

Saturday
The Ministry of Reconciliation
(2 Corinthians 5:6-21)

Memory Verses

Romans 1:16

Romans 3:22,23

Chapter 2

God's Power to Save

Introduction: Paul's eagerness to tell the Good News, to preach the gospel to the Gentiles, was motivated by his recognition of our separation from God because of sin. No one could deny that he had sinned without making God a liar (1 John 1:10). That includes me. It includes you. What power can free me from sin's stranglehold on my life? Paul identifies that power; he is anxious to share it with the Romans . . . and with us:

> *I am under obligation both to Greeks and to barbarians, both to the wise and to the foolish: so I am eager to preach the gospel to you also who are in Rome. For I am not ashamed of the gospel: it is the power of God for salvation to every one who has faith, to the Jew first and also to the Greek. For in it the righteousness of God is revealed through faith for faith; as it is written, "He who through faith is righteous shall live" (Romans 1:14-17, RSV).*

I. My electric typewriter is useless when it is not connected to its source of power, the electrical outlet. The power is there, within inches, but the cord must be plugged in! The same is true of the gospel; it is available to all nations, but each individual must "make connection" with the power available through the gospel. This is not quite so simple as plugging in a typewriter, but God's Word tells us just what the "Good News" is, what it can do for us, and how to obtain its benefits in our own lives.

   A. Perhaps the best definition of the gospel is given by Paul in his letter to the Corinthians:

> *Now, brothers, I want to remind you of the gospel I preached to you, which you received and on which you have taken your stand. By this gospel you are saved, if you hold firmly to the word*

I preached to you. Otherwise you have believed in vain. For what I received I passed on to you as of first importance: that Christ died for our sins according to the Scriptures, that he was buried, that he was raised on the third day according to the Scriptures, and that he appeared to Peter and then to the Twelve (1 Corinthians 15:1-5, NIV).

What is the gospel, the Good News, then? It is that Christ died for our sins, that He was buried, and that He arose on the third day. These things had been foretold by the scriptures. The resurrection was confirmed by eyewitnesses—first Peter, then the Twelve. Paul goes on to say that Christ appeared to more than 500 of the brothers, some of whom still were living at the time of Paul's writing of this epistle. He adds that Christ also appeared to James and finally—on the road to Damascus—to Paul himself "as of one born out of due time." Although the Roman soldiers spread the story that Christ's body was stolen away by His followers, His resurrection from the dead was given infallible proof by these appearances. Paul affirms the significance of Christ's resurrection as he concludes: "For as in Adam all die, even so in Christ shall all be made alive" (1 Corinthians 15:22, KJ).

Note in the above scripture that we are told, "By this gospel you are saved." But there was a condition: the hearers were to hold firmly to the word Paul had preached to them. It was even possible that their belief was in vain if they did not respond to what they had been taught. What was the divine plan for the salvation of sinners by the gospel?

B. Repeatedly, we read that the gospel is to be preached not just to the Jews, but to all nations. Jesus warned His apostles that they could expect to be persecuted, to be brought before rulers and kings for His sake. Apparently, these persecutions would be a means of the spread of the gospel, for He said, "And the gospel must first be preached to all nations" (Mark 13:10, RSV). Then just before His ascension, He charged them, "Go into all the world and preach the gospel to the whole creation" (Mark 16:15, RSV).

Over and over in his epistles, Paul refers to the gospel, stressing its importance in God's plan. It is mentioned six times in the first chapter, including his declaration that he serves God with his whole heart in preaching the gospel of His Son (verse 9). Then in 1 Corinthians 9:16 he says, "Yet when I preach the gospel, I cannot boast, for I am compelled to preach. Woe to me if I do not preach the gospel!" His calling was to spread the Good News and to share in its blessings, not the least of which was his joy in seeing those he taught "begotten by the gospel." We might say that God's saving power through the gospel, literally the Good News, is Paul's theme throughout his letter to the Romans, for in

20

his concluding remarks he confirms, "God is the One who can make you strong in faith. God can use the Good News that I teach to make you strong. That is the Good News about Jesus Christ that I tell people. That Good News is the secret truth that God has made known . . . And that secret truth has been made known to all people, so that they can believe and obey God" (Romans 16:25b-26d, ERV).

C. Paul rejoiced in the success of the gospel in its saving power, but it was his unhappy task to warn some that the gospel could be perverted. We homemakers know that a little pollution can spoil perfectly good food; the same is true of the gospel. Some have asked, "Why so many churches?" The obvious answer is that the gospel has been polluted by the doctrines of men. Jesus warned, "In vain they do worship me, teaching for doctrines the commandments of men" (Matthew 15:9, KJ).

Because of denominational division today, we can understand Paul's concern when he had to warn the Galatians:

> A short time ago, God called you to follow him. He called you through his grace **(kindness)** that came through Christ. But now I am amazed at you people! You are already turning away and believing a different gospel. Really, there is no other true gospel. But some people are confusing you. They want to change the gospel of Christ. We told you the true gospel. So if we ourselves or even an angel from heaven tells you a different gospel, he should be condemned! I said this before. Now I say it again: You have already accepted the true gospel. If any person tells you another way to be saved, he should be condemned! (Galatians 1:6-9, ERV).

D. When people of any nation obey the gospel, they are saved. If they refuse or neglect to obey, they are condemned. Paul wrote the Ephesians, "And you also were included in Christ when you heard the word of truth, the gospel of our salvation" (Ephesians 1:13a, NIV). We will see later how Paul equates being saved to being in Christ.

After praising the Thessalonian Christians for their faith, love and endurance, Paul assured them that those who were troubling them would be punished: "The Lord Jesus will be revealed from heaven with his powerful angels. He will come with a flaming fire. He will punish the people who do not acknowledge God and those who don't obey the gospel of our Lord Jesus. They will be punished with eternal destruction—away from the Lord and from the glory of his strength" (2 Thessalonians 1:7b-9, SEB).

21

We see that the gospel is the Good News that Jesus Christ died for our sins, was buried, and that His resurrection was manifested to many witnesses. He gave instruction to His apostles that the gospel was to be preached to all nations, to every creature. Paul devoted his life to the proclamation of the gospel and warned that there were some who would pervert the gospel. In obedience to the gospel we can be saved, but terrible punishment awaits those who do not obey, those who preach false doctrine.

II. We must never lose sight of the fact that Jesus Christ is our Savior, but we have seen conclusively that certain things are required in obedience to the gospel. The choice is ours. We can obey and be saved or disobey and join the devil and his angels in destruction. Just as a doctor uses medicine as a means to heal, the gospel is Christ's means to salvation.

A. In Romans 5, we noted that Paul says we are justified by faith, but we noted also that one could believe in vain. So how are we assured of saving faith? In the following chapter we read, "But thanks be to God, that you who were once slaves to sin have become obedient from the heart to the standard of teaching to which you were committed, and having been set free from sin, have become slaves of righteousness" (Romans 6:17,18, RSV).

Faith is produced by hearing God's Word; so a part of the teaching the Romans had been given was that the Word, when heard, produces faith. We may believe what our parents taught us and claim that as our faith, or we may believe what we hear on the radio or see on television and claim that as saving faith; but we do not really have a faith that will lead us to saving obedience until we listen to what God has said through the inspired writers. That word is available even to those who cannot read it for themselves today through tapes and players within the means of a limited budget. We can hear! Paul informs us, "So then faith cometh by hearing and hearing by the word of God" (Romans 10:17, KJ).

Having heard or read the word of God for ourselves, we can be "sure of the things we hope for" and "know that something is real if we don't see it" (Hebrews 11:1). Then we have the faith without which it is impossible to please God (Hebrews 11:6).

B. Having faith based on the Word, we will want to serve God; therefore, we will be sorry for our sins and determine to turn from our old way of life and dedicate ourselves to Christ. Suppose you are making a dress. You sew a sleeve in backward. Either by reading the pattern or being shown by one who knows, you must be convinced you did the wrong thing. You rip out the seam, determined this time to follow the pattern. This is repentance; you realize you have been wrong and resolve in your heart that you will do right.

Just as a loving, patient mother may have taught you how to correct your mistake in sewing, our loving heavenly Father, through His kindness, wants to lead us to repentance. Paul upbraided those who were doing the things they condemned in others, perhaps thinking they would escape God's judgment. He added, "Or do you presume upon the riches of his kindness and forebearance and patience? Do you not know that God's kindness is meant to lead you to repentance?" (Romans 2:4, RSV).

There is sorrow that does not lead to repentance. We may be sorry that our sin has been discovered, but we do not determine that we will not sin willfully again. Paul made the Corinthians sad by his first letter, but he was not sorry that he had written, because his letter produced godly sorrow on their part which led to their repentance: "I am glad now, not because you were sad, but because you were sad enough to change your hearts! . . . The kind of sorrow which God uses brings a change of heart that leads to salvation" (2 Corinthians 7:9a,10, SEB).

Jesus said, "Repent or perish" (Luke 13:3). We have a choice. Our sorrow can lead us to a change of heart, or we can harden our heart and continue in our own willful way to destruction.

C. We who have been reared in Christian homes have been taught from early childhood that Jesus Christ is the promised messiah. We always have believed that He is the son of God. Therefore, to confess that fact is easy for us, but we may not be aware always of that confession's implication of commitment. It was not so easy for those early Christians who realized that their entire life would be changed because many of the religious leaders of that day were the strongest enemies of Jesus. To accept Christ was to go against their traditional religions, chiefly the Pharisees and Sadducees. Because of Paul's confession of Christ, his former allies became his enemies and plotted to kill him.

Many people today are taught to believe in a prophet other than Jesus Christ. If they accept Him as their Lord, they too will be cut off from their earthly families. It is they who need careful teaching from the four gospels in order to lead them to believe in Christ and to confess and obey Him.

In Paul's dealing with the subject of confession in Romans 10, he still is showing that Christ's way of faith is superior to, and has supplanted, the law of Moses:

> Brothers, my deepest desire and my prayer to God is for their salvation. To their zeal for God I can testify; but it is an ill-formed zeal. For they ignore God's way of righteousness, and try to set up

23

their own, and therefore they have not submitted themselves to God's righteousness. For Christ ends the law and brings righteousness for everyone who has faith.

Of legal righteousness Moses writes, "The man who does this shall gain life by it." But the righteousness that comes by faith says, "Do not say to yourself, 'Who can go up to heaven?' (that is to bring Christ down) or 'Who can go down to the abyss?' (to bring Christ up from the dead). But what does it say? The word is near you: it is upon your lips and in your heart." This means the word of faith which we proclaim. If on your lips is the confession, "Jesus is Lord," and in your heart the faith that God raised him from the dead, then you will find salvation. For the faith that leads to righteousness is in the heart, and the confession that leads to salvation is upon the lips (Romans 10:1-10, NEB).

Please note confession on the lips and the faith in the heart lead one to find salvation; neither is an end in itself but will prompt the confessed believer to do what is necessary to be saved.

John tells us that many who heard Jesus' teaching did not believe in spite of having seen Him perform miracles. "Nevertheless among the chief rulers also many believed on him; but because of the Pharisees they did not confess him, lest they should be put out of the synagogue: For they loved the praise of men more than the praise of God" (John 12:42,43, KJ).

Are you going to be like those people and fail to confess Christ because of man's religion or social pressures, or would you like to broadcast to the world, "Jesus is **my** Lord!"? You may not confess Him now, but the time will come when even the Pharisaical leaders will join everyone in confessing Him as Lord: "And being found in human form he humbled himself and became obedient unto death, even death on a cross. Therefore God has highly exalted him and bestowed on him the name which is above every name, that at the name of Jesus every knee should bow, in heaven and on earth and under the earth, and every tongue confess that Jesus Christ is Lord, to the glory of God the Father" (Philippians 2:8-11, RSV).

III. When you are taking a family trip, perhaps the question heard most often from children is, "How much farther?" To be able to answer that question accurately, we watch the highway signs, noting with satisfaction as the mileage dwindles from hundreds to only five or ten miles. As we take the steps **unto** salvation, we are getting closer and closer to our goal. Although through a final step we are born into Christ and saved from our past sins, we will see in lessons to come that the road to our final destination—eternal life with God, Christ, and all the saved—is marked just as well as are our steps into a covenant relationship with God through Christ.

Paul identifies baptism as the step which takes us into Christ: "Have you forgotten that when we were baptized into union with Christ Jesus we were baptized into his death? By baptism we were buried with him, and lay dead, in order that, as Christ was raised from the dead in the splendour of the Father, so also we might set our feet upon the new path of life" (Romans 6:3,4, NEB). Also, in Galatians 3:27 he cites baptism as the way into Christ.

A. If all had followed the path taken by translators of *The Simple English Bible,* we could have avoided the confusion in the religious world in identifying Bible baptism. They refused to follow the custom of transliteration, whereby the Greek words *baptizo* and *baptisma* were simply adapted to the English language. Instead, they gave them an accurate **translation: immerse** and **immersion**. They read, in the above passage, "**immersed** into Christ . . . through **immersion**, we were buried with him into death."

In his dictionary of New Testament words, W. E. Vine gives the meaning of *baptisma* as "baptism, consisting of the process of immersion, submersion, and emergence," and says that it is used in both John's and Christian baptism.* He defines *baptizo* as **to dip**, used among the Greeks to signify the dyeing of a garment, or the drawing of water by dipping a vessel into another, etc. . . . the baptism enjoined by Christ, Matthew 28:19, a baptism to be undergone by believers, thus witnessing to their identification with Him in death, burial and resurrection."*

We find no discussion of the **mode** of baptism in the New Testament simply because it was understood that the baptism being taught by Jesus and His disciples was immersion in water. Sprinkling was introduced at a much later date in the guise of "clinical baptism," which it was felt could be administered more easily and safely to those who were ill. Pouring is also considered by some to be a more convenient way to baptize. Some consider it a beautiful ceremony when a preacher dips a rose in water and sprinkles it on the head of perhaps a sleeping or crying infant—certainly one who has not heard the Word and believed, has no sins of which to be repentant, as prerequisites to scriptural baptism. We pray that these remarks will not offend you; but if they do, we pray earnestly that you will be prompted to a careful examination of the scriptural teaching on baptism. If, as the passage above indicates, im-

* W. E. Vine, *An Expository Dictionary of New Testament Words,* Fleming H. Revell Company, Old Tappan, New Jersey, 1940, pages 96 and 97.

25

mersion in water is the **door** through which we enter the body of Christ, do we dare consider it so unimportant that we ignore the scriptural teaching on the subject? What would your reaction be if I came to your house and said, "Yes, I'd like to come in, but I won't come in through the door. I'd prefer to climb through a window." Jesus said, "I am the door; if any one enters by me, he will be saved" (John 10:9, RSV).

According to Ephesians 1:3, God has blessed us with all spiritual blessings **in Christ**. If all spiritual blessings are in Christ, then we must be in Christ to receive those blessings. Let's look again at Galatians 3:27: "For as many of you as have been baptized into Christ have put on Christ" (KJ).

Some very sincere and respectable religious groups teach that baptism has nothing to do with one's salvation, but that it is an indication that one **has been** saved. After citing the salvation of Noah's family in the ark by water, Peter wrote, "Baptism, which corresponds to this, now saves you, not as a removal of dirt from the body, but as an appeal to God for a clear conscience, through the resurrection of Jesus Christ" (1 Peter 3:21, RSV).

After studying for some time with a woman who had been a member of a denomination which teaches that baptism has nothing to do with salvation, my husband turned to this scripture and asked her to read it.

"You are saying that I have not been saved," she commented.

"It is not what I say that affects your salvation," he replied. "Please read the scripture again. What does the Bible say to you?"

"I am not a Christian!" she said after reading and rereading the passage, thinking seriously. Then she added, "When can I be baptized?"

She was baptized and spent the rest of her life being just a Christian, doing her very best to do just what her Lord wanted her to do. She knew the peace of being free from doubt. That assurance is available to everyone who will study God's Word with a good and honest heart.

     B. Now that we have learned that baptism is an immersion and that it puts us into Christ, let's consider why each of us must be willing to submit to it.

     1. Just before His ascension into heaven, Jesus gave what is known as the "great commission":

> *The eleven followers went to a mountain in Galilee where Jesus had told them to meet him. When they saw him, they worshiped him, but some had doubts. Jesus came to them and said, "All authority in heaven and on earth has been given to me. Therefore, after you've gone out, make followers for me from all nations. Immerse them by the authority of the Father, the Son,*

and the Holy Spirit. *Teach them to obey everything I commanded you. Remember, I will always be with you—even until the end of time (Matthew 28:16-20, SEB).*

The apostles were to teach all nations; their immersion was by the authority of the divine trinity to make disciples for Jesus. Those who were baptized then were to be taught to continue to obey the commands which Jesus was transmitting through the apostles.

In Mark's account of the great commission, we read, "Jesus said to them, 'When you have gone into the whole world, preach the Good News to all mankind. The person who believes it and is immersed will be saved, but the person who doesn't believe it will be condemned' " (Mark 16:15,16, SEB).

Note, the person who **believes** and **is immersed** will be saved. The argument has been made that baptism, or immersion, is not essential because condemnation was pronounced only on those who do not believe. Suppose you tell your daughter that she may watch *Sesame Street* if she cleans her room and empties the trash. Suppose she cleans her room but does not empty the trash—will you allow her to watch her favorite program? She met one of the conditions, but not the other. Too, **and** is a coordinating conjunction, joining things of equal importance. Belief is also a prerequisite of baptism. Philip told the Ethiopian eunuch, "If you believe, you may" (Acts 8:37).

2. In the book of Acts, we see God's power at work through the gospel. We read of the first converts and the establishment of the church in Acts 2. All the apostles preached, and people heard in their own language after the promised outpouring of the Holy Spirit on the twelve. Peter's sermon is recorded in part. He quoted prophecy and referred to Jesus' teaching and miracles to convince his hearers that Jesus was the Son of God. We read:

"Therefore all the people of Israel can be sure of this one thing: God has made Jesus both Lord and Messiah, this man whom you nailed to the cross!"

When the people heard this, they felt a sharp, cutting pain in their conscience. They asked Peter and the other apostles, "What should we do, brothers?"

Then Peter answered, "Change your hearts and each one of you must be immersed by the authority of Jesus the Messiah, so that your sins may be forgiven. Then you will receive the gift of the Holy Spirit. This promise is for you and for your children. It is also for people who are far away, for everyone whom the Lord our God may call" . . . *Then those people who accepted what Peter said were immersed. On that day, about 3,000 people were added to the group of believers (Acts 2:36-39,41, SEB).*

We could continue through the book of Acts noting that the apostles and other disciples went everywhere, preaching the Word. We read of the Ethiopian eunuch in Acts 8; of Cornelius, the first Gentile convert, in Acts 10; and of Lydia and the Philippian jailer in Acts 16. These are only a few of the recorded conversions, all of which end with the believer's baptism. We must conclude, therefore, that baptism is the culmination of the process of salvation from past sins—that it is the act which puts one into Christ.

Conclusion: Paul presents the gospel as God's power at work to free those in bondage to sin and allow them to live a new life in Christ Jesus. He describes that new life beautifully:

> *Christ died, and we have been joined with Christ by dying too. So we will also be joined with him by rising from death like Christ rose from death. We know that our old life died with Christ on the cross. This happened so that our sinful selves would have no power over us. And then we would not be slaves to sin. Any person who has died is made free from sin's control (**power**).*
>
> *If we died with Christ, we know that we will also live with him. Christ was raised from death. And we know that he cannot die again. Death has no power over him now. Yes, when Christ died, he died to **defeat the power** of sin one time—enough for all time. He now has a new life, and his new life is with God. In the same way, you should see yourselves as being dead to the power of sin. And see yourselves as being alive for God through Christ Jesus (Romans 6:5-11, ERV).*

How great! Alive for God! The Christian life is not a dull, dreary life. Those who have obeyed the gospel are ready to start really living!

Daily Bible Reading

Sunday
The Gospel Defined
(1 Corinthians 15:1-5)

Monday
Don't Pervert the Gospel
(Galatians 1:6-9,11)

Tuesday
Life Through the Word
(Psalm 119:33-48)

Wednesday
Faith
(Hebrews 11:1-40)

Thursday
Godly Sorrow and Repentance
(2 Corinthians 7:8-11)

Friday
Confession That Leads to Salvation
(Romans 10:1-10)

Saturday
A Birthday (of the Church)
and 3,000 Babes in Christ
(Acts 2:1-47)

Memory Verses

Romans 10:9,10,17

Matthew 28:18-20

Acts 2:38

Chapter 3

A New Path

Introduction: We have seen that obedience to the gospel puts us into Christ and sets our feet upon the new path of life, walking in newness of life on a higher plane (Romans 6:3,4). Whatever in our old way of life had separated us from God was eliminated as we enacted a figure of Jesus Christ's death, burial, and resurrection when we went down into the waters of baptism and were buried and arose a new person: "If any person is in Christ, then that person is made new. The old things have gone; everything is made new!" (2 Corinthians 5:17, ERV).

In studying Romans, Chapters 6 through 11, we see that the new path leads to life and peace **if** we allow the Spirit to control our thinking rather than being controlled by our sinful, carnal nature (Romans 8:6). We must be "poor in spirit"—that is, we must recognize continually our dependence on God and His provision for the help we need in those times when we want to do good but lack the power to resist temptation.

    I. **We need help** all along the way! Just as we were able to escape the shackles of sin through our primary obedience to the gospel, we see our continual need in Paul's putting himself in our place in his struggle between being a slave to sin or alive to God.

        A. "The law is spiritual, but I am carnal, sold under sin," Paul cried, almost in desperation (Romans 7:14).

Have you ever had to say, "Now, **why** did I do that?"

Welcome to the club! Sometimes we are looking for a way to blame someone else. But at other times of mature perplexity, it is hard for us to see how we could have done something so contrary to our own principles. Perhaps Paul's conflict can shed light on our own:

> *I don't understand the things I do. I don't do the **good** things I want to do. And I do the **bad** things I hate to do. And if I don't want to do the **bad** things I do, then that means that I agree that*

31

*the law is good. But it is not really me that is doing these **bad** things. It is sin living in me that does these things. Yes, I know that nothing good lives in me—I mean nothing good lives in the part of me that is earthly and sinful. I want to do the things that are good. But I don't do those things. I don't do the good things that I want to do. I do the bad things that I don't want to do (Romans 7:15-19, ERV).*

    B. In other words, the fight is not over when we become Christians. We belong to Christ, and our purpose is to be used in His service. But just as God is alive and working in our lives, Satan too is alive. Peter pictures him as an ever-present danger: "Control yourselves and be careful! The devil is your enemy. And he goes around like a roaring lion looking for some person to eat. Refuse to follow the devil. Stand strong in your faith" (1 Peter 5:8,9a, ERV). Another translation says, "Resist him, firm in your faith" (RSV).

Our old associate, the things we once did when we were servants of sin, all that is in the world—the lust of the flesh, the lust of the eyes, and the pride of life—may work even harder to drag us back to the old life. We should never be too proud to seek help from the spiritually mature. We know that this is one way that God's help is made available to us. Like Paul, we must see the situation as it really is:

*So I have learned this rule: When I want to do good, evil is there with me. In my mind, I am happy with God's law. But I see another law working in my body. That law makes war against the law that my mind accepts. That other law working in my body is the law of sin, and that law makes me its prisoner. This is terrible! Who will save me from this body that brings me death? God **will save me!** I thank him **for his salvation** through Jesus Christ our Lord! (Romans 7:21-24, ERV).*

    II. Those who have known the burden of sin experience such great peace when they are relieved of their burden that they gladly dedicate their total being to **a life of righteousness**. The angels in heaven rejoice with other Christians when they witness the transforming power of the gospel. We join Paul in saying, "But thanks be to God, that you who were once slaves of sin have become obedient from the heart to the standard of teaching to which you were committed, and, having been set free from sin, have become slaves of righteousness" (Romans 8:17,18, RSV).

Those thus dedicated to Christ face **no condemnation** so long as they do not walk according to the flesh but according to the spirit (Romans 8:1-4).

A. Those who walk after the flesh are condemned. In the first chapter of this series, we noted Paul's description of the sinful life; he prefaced that description with the assertion that there really is no excuse for such a life of sin and rebellion. God has made His will known not only through His recorded Word, but also in the things God has made.

Later, he pictures the sinful life as selfish:

> People who live following their sinful selves think only about things that their sinful selves want. But those people who live following the Spirit are thinking about the things that the Spirit wants them to do. If a person's thinking is controlled by his sinful self, then there is spiritual death. But if a person's thinking is controlled by the Spirit, then there is life and peace. Why is this true? Because if a person's thinking is controlled by his sinful self, then that person is against God. That person refuses to obey God's law. And really that person is not able to obey God's law. Those people who are ruled by their sinful selves cannot please God (Romans 8:5-8, ERV).

Jesus, too, had made it clear that a person's sinful life is a result of an impure heart, evil thoughts:

> But the bad things a person says with his mouth come from the way a person thinks. And these are the things that make a person wrong. All these bad things begin in a person's mind: evil thoughts, murder, adultery, sexual sins, stealing, lying, saying bad things against other people. These things make a person wrong (Matthew 15:18-20a, ERV).

B. Those who walk according to the Spirit are free from the condemnation pronounced on those described above. They are free from the law of sin and death, for the law of the Spirit of life in Christ Jesus has set them free (Romans 8:2). God made this possible by sending His son as an offering for sin. In our previous lesson, we saw how God chose to take alien sinners and make of them members of Christ's body, in which they can experience an abundant, righteous life. They enjoy a perpetual cleansing: "God is the light. We should also live in light. If we live in the light, then we have a relationship of sharing with each other, and the blood of Jesus, God's son, continues to cleanse us from all sin" (1 John 1:7, SEB). Thus, walking according to the Spirit is continuing faithfully in fellowship with God's people, where we receive renewal through study of God's Word, prayer, spiritual songs, the opportunity to give of ourselves and our means, and communion around the Lord's Table. This provides strength for a life in the Spirit through-out our days, from week to week, for a lifetime.

III. The spiritual life assures **no complications**. Certainly, there will be difficulties, but we will have the strength to face and over-come them through God's power working in us.

A. God can make good out of what seems bad to us. We are told, "And we know that all things work together for good to them that love God, to them that are called according to his purpose" (Romans 8:28, KJ).

That God's hand is in this working is perhaps made clearer in another translation: "We know that in everything God works for the good of those people who love him. These are the people God called *(chose)*, because that was his plan" (Romans 8:28, ERV).

In trying, with our finite minds, to understand just **how** God works, are we in danger of violating one of Paul's "don'ts"? He wrote the Thes-salonians, "Quench not the Spirit" (KJ). That translates easily, as in *The Simple English Bible,* to "Don't put out **the fire** of the Spirit."

Paul prayed for the Ephesians: "That he would grant you, according to the riches of his glory, to be strengthened with might by his Spirit in the inner man" (Ephesians 3:16, KJ). Does this not indicate that the Spirit is the means God uses, within us, to give us strength?

The conclusion of that chapter, and thought, from another version reads, "With God's power working in us, God can do much, much more than anything we can ask or think of. To him be glory in the church and in Christ Jesus for all time, for ever and ever. Amen" (Ephe-sians 3:20,21, ERV). Other translations, from King James to the most modern, agree with these in picturing to us a power working within us by the Holy Spirit, from God, that is greater than we could ever dare to ask or imagine.

B. In addition to this awe-inspiring help from God, we also have the Son whom, through His great love, He gave to die for us. We are told that Jesus is pleading our cause before His Father:

What then shall we say to this? If God is for us, who is against us? He who did not spare his own Son but gave him up for us all, will he not also give us all things with him? Who shall bring any charge against God's elect? Is it Christ Jesus, who died, yes, who was raised from the dead, who is at the right hand of God, who indeed intercedes for us? (Romans 8:31-34, RSV).

C. Have there been times when you did not know how to express your need to God in prayer? Help is available! The Holy Spirit understands our plight and conveys our message to God in an ap-proved manner:

We don't know how we should pray, but the Spirit helps our weakness. He personally talks to God for us with feelings which OUR language cannot express. God searches ALL MEN'S hearts. He knows what the Spirit is thinking. The Spirit talks to God in behalf of holy people, using the manner which pleases God (Romans 8:26,27, SEB).

Complications too big to be handled? With a team like **that**! Would you **dare** try to make it alone?

IV. With God's help, we need fear **no separation**! Perhaps a small child's greatest fear is being separated from his mother. Indeed we should, above all else, be afraid of eternal separation from God. In another epistle, Paul informs us that just such a separation awaits those who do not know God and do not obey the gospel: "Those people will be punished with a destruction that continues forever. They will not be allowed to be with the Lord" (2 Thessalonians 1:9, ERV).

The above scripture does not mean, however, that you as a child of God should live a trembling, fearful life, always afraid you may fall. A child secure in his mother's love can play happily in his room as he hears his mother singing while she goes about her daily tasks. We have seen that God, Christ, and the Holy Spirit stand ready to help us overcome complications in our lives. We may, like a wandering child at the fair, leave them, but they will not leave us so long as we walk in the light. Nothing else can separate us from their love:

Can anything separate us from the love of Christ? No! Can trouble separate us from Christ's love? No! Can problems or persecution separate us from Christ's love? No! If we have no food or clothes, will that separate us from Christ's love? No! Will danger or even death separate us from Christ's love? No! (Romans 8:35, ERV).

A. God made and loves us. He extends mercy to sinners who seek Him with all their hearts; He lends strength, not only through the Spirit in the inner man, but also through His ministering servants; through Jesus Christ, we have access to God's grace.

1. Through the prophets, God warned the Israelites repeatedly of the troubles which would come upon them if they failed to obey His commands and turned to idols. Yet in Moses' address to them before they entered Canaan, the assurance is given that they still could reach Him, and at least a remnant would be shown His great mercy:

And the Lord will scatter you among the peoples, and you will be left few in number among the nations where the Lord will drive you. And there you will serve gods of wood and stone, the work

35

of men's hands, that neither see, nor hear, nor eat, nor smell. But from there you will seek the Lord your God, and you will find him, if you search after him with all your heart and with all your soul. When you are in tribulation, and all these things come upon you in the latter days, you will return to the Lord your God and obey his voice, for the Lord your God is a merciful God; he will not fail you or destroy you or forget the covenant with your fathers which he swore to them (Deuteronomy 4:27-31, RSV).

God's mercy is available to us today on the same terms. We must seek Him sincerely. Only our willful disobedience will separate us from Him. Even then, He will have mercy on us if we repent (with all our heart look for the way back and promise ourselves that we will do His will).

        2. Paul and Barnabas learned that troubles may come because of fickle human nature. Both Jews and Greeks in large numbers responded to their preaching of the gospel in Iconium. But the unbelieving Jews, just like those who were chief persecutors of Christ, stirred up and poisoned the minds of the Gentiles against the apostles. Notwithstanding, they continued to preach boldly, using signs and miracles God allowed them to use to confirm their words. Some of the non-believers, both Jews and non-Jews, attempted to molest and stone them, and they fled to Lystra.

Again, we see typical human nature at work. When the apostles caused a lame man to walk, the people tried to worship them, calling them gods. Even after assuring the emotional crowd that they were only men, tools in the hand of God to bring them the Good News of Christ, it was almost impossible to keep the people from offering sacrifices to them. How quickly that ardor turned to hate when Jews from Antioch and Iconium came down and were able to turn them against the speakers. They stoned Paul and drug him out of the city, supposing he was dead. Surrounded by the disciples, he arose and went into the city, then on to Derbe with Barnabas. Did they avoid the cities where they had suffered such persecution? Let's see:

When they had preached the gospel in that city and had made many disciples, they returned to Lystra, to Iconium and to Antioch, strengthening the souls of the disciples, exhorting them to continue in the faith, and saying that through many tribulations we must enter the kingdom of God. And when they had appointed elders in every church, with prayer and fasting, they committed them to the Lord in whom they believed (Acts 14:21-23, RSV).

Not only did Paul and Barnabas demonstrate a faith in God that was able to face persecution, even death—they lent their own encouragement to those disciples who had remained faithful in spite of trouble. They carried further God's plan for helping believers by appointing elders—shepherds, pastors—to watch after their souls.

3. With access to God's grace, through Jesus Christ, we can be happy about our troubles! Good can come from them:

We have been made right with God because of our faith. So we have peace with God through our Lord Jesus Christ. Through our faith, Christ has brought us into that blessing of God's grace **(kindness)** *that we now enjoy. And we are very happy because of the hope we have of sharing God's glory. And we are also happy with the troubles we have. Why are we happy with troubles? Because we know that these troubles make us more patient. And this patience is proof that we are strong. And this proof gives us hope. And this hope will never disappoint us—it will never fail. Why? Because God has poured out his love to fill our hearts. God gave us his love through the Holy Spirit. That Holy Spirit was a gift to us from God . . . Christ died for us while we were still sinners. In that way, God showed us that he loves us very much (Romans 5:1-5,8, ERV).*

Troubles, problems, and persecution **cannot** separate us from the love and providence of God! His love is manifested to us not only by His sending Christ and the Holy Spirit, but also in the love and concern of our fellow Christians.

B. Need we be separated from God by our physical needs? No! In His sermon on the mount, Jesus made it quite clear that our heavenly Father is aware of temporal needs and will see that they are supplied:

You cannot serve God and money **at the same time.** *Because of this, I am telling you, you should not worry about what you will eat to stay alive. DON'T WORRY about what clothes you will wear. Living is more important than eating, and the body is more important than clothes. Look at the wild birds of the sky. Birds do not plant seeds or harvest them or gather them into barns, but your heavenly Father takes care of them. Are you not worth so much more than birds? Of course! None of you can grow 18 inches taller by worrying about it. And why worry about clothes? Learn from the way the wild flowers grow. They do not work hard or make threads for clothes. I tell you, even Solomon, with all his beautiful clothes, was not dressed as well as one of* *these flowers. Look how well God clothes the grass in the fields! But grass is here today and thrown into the oven tomorrow to be burned. Will not God dress you so much better? Oh, you have so little faith!*

So don't worry, thinking to yourself, "What will we eat?" or "What will we drink?" or "What will we wear?" People without God put all these things first. Your heavenly Father knows you need all these things. So, put first God's kingdom and what is right. Then all the **things** *you need will be given to you (Matthew 6:24c-33, SEB).*

Does this mean that we are simply to sit down and let God, the government, or others feed and clothe us? Hardly! The key is in seeking God's kingdom first; then provision will be made for our physical needs. We learn in 1 Timothy 5 that God expects Christians to provide for their own households. I have told junior-age girls that Jesus did not mean, either, that God would provide each of us a Cadillac, a wide-screen television, or many of the unnecessary things about which we are concerned.

Provision is made through the Lord's church to provide necessities for those who are not able to do so for themselves. A good example is the Christian Service Center, through which Christians give food and clothing to those in Tulsa and the area who need physical help. At the same time, an attempt is made by loving followers of Christ to fill their needs for spiritual food. Tons of clothing and food have been pooled in disaster areas and distributed by Christians to relieve suffering and want, to the glory of the Lord. Struggling congregations have been strengthened, and many have been led to Christ through those who ministered in the name of Christ to physical needs.

C. Neither suffering, danger, nor death will separate us from Christ's love. Those whose trust is truly in the Lord can rise above circumstance and live happy, useful lives.

After being thrown into prison, Peter and the other apostles were commanded not to speak further in the name of Jesus. Peter declared, "We must obey God rather than men" (Acts 5:29, RSV). He then recounted how Jesus, whom those very religious leaders had killed, had been raised from the dead and exalted at God's right hand as Prince and Savior. The Jewish leaders were so enraged they wanted to kill the apostles, but were dissuaded by Gamaliel. They did beat them and commanded them again not to speak in Christ's name.

"Then they left the presence of the council, rejoicing that they were counted worthy to suffer for the name. And every day in the temple and at home they did not cease teaching and preaching Jesus as the Christ" (Acts 5:41,42, RSV).

Stephen, the first Christian martyr, declared boldly that just as their fathers had killed the prophets whom God sent to warn them, the Jewish leaders to whom he was speaking had turned against Jesus, the righteous one, and had murdered Him. They became so angry that they took him outside the city and stoned him to death. While he was being stoned, he looked up into heaven and saw Jesus standing at God's right hand. Just as Jesus had prayed for those who crucified Him, Stephen prayed, "Lord, do not hold this sin against them" (Acts 7:60).

Being "faithful unto death" can mean actually dying for Christ. But it may also mean being dead to self and to sin, living for Jesus.

"You have died, and your life is hid with Christ in God," Paul wrote the Colossians (Colossians 3:3). Of himself he declared, "I have been crucified with Christ; it is no longer I who live, but Christ who lives in me; and the life I now live in the flesh I live by faith in the Son of God, who loved me and gave himself for me" (Galatians 2:20, RSV).

Thus, we see that dying with or for Christ is not separation from, but complete union with, Him. Paul saw living as an opportunity to exalt Christ and dying as advantage, because he would be with Christ:

> The thing I want and hope for is that I will not fail Christ in anything. I hope that I will have the courage now, like always, to show the greatness of Christ in my life here on earth. I want to do that if I die or if I live. I mean that to me the only important thing about living is Christ. And even death would be profit for me, **because death would bring me nearer to Christ** (Philippians 1:20,21, ERV).

D. You and I can achieve Paul's spiritual maturity, his freedom from fear of whatever faced him, when we are as confident as he was of God's love as expressed to us in Christ Jesus. He had achieved the perfect love, proved by obedience, described by John: "There is no fear in love, because perfect love casts out fear. For fear has to do with punishment, and he who fears is not perfected in love" (1 John 4:18, RSV).

Therefore, Paul was able to see Christians as "more than conquerors":

> But in all these things we have full victory through God who showed his love for us. Yes, I am sure that nothing can separate us from the love of God. Not death, not life, not angels, not ruling spirits, nothing now or in the future, no powers, nothing above

39

us, nothing below us, or anything else in the whole world will ever
be able to separate us from the love of God that is in Christ Jesus
our Lord (Romans 8:37-39, ERV).

V. Remember Paul's plea that we present our bodies as living
sacrifices? Beginning in the first chapter of Romans, he pictured the
extreme sinfulness of man. It was so terrible that it made God angry.
But he then began to show us the magnitude of God's grace, extended
to both Jew and Gentile. He did not repudiate the law of Moses, but he
did show that it was a means to bring mankind to the promised Christ.
Gentiles were being brought to Christ because of their faith. Some of the
Jews, following their traditions imposed on the law, had stumbled as the
prophets had said they would: "And the people of Israel tried to follow
a law to make themselves right with God. But they did not suc-
ceed. Why not? Because they tried to make themselves right by the
things they did. They did not trust God to make them right" (Romans
9:32a, ERV).

A. God's grace is available to people of every nation
through the gospel, which Jesus told His disciples to preach to every
creature. Early in this century, when human rights had not advanced,
even in the Lord's church, to the oblivion of racial prejudice toward
which we are striving still, I am told that Brother Marshall Keeble said,
"I cannot be denied access to my Lord because of my race. There are
some who may think I am not *human*, but they cannot deny that I am a
creature. Jesus commanded that the gospel be preached even to *me!*"

Paul was dealing with prejudice among the Jews toward the Gentiles
that was just as volatile then as race relations have been during this century in America. The Jews had boasted, arrogantly, to Christ that they
were descendants of Abraham, heirs to the promise. Much of the ninth
and tenth chapters of Romans are spent in destroying that fallacy.
He declared, "This means that not all of Abraham's descendants
(**family**) are God's true children. Abraham's true children are those
people that become God's children because of the promise God made
to Abraham" (Romans 9:8, ERV).

In the previous chapter, Paul had given a very clear definition of
those who have the honor of being called "children of God":

> People who follow human nature are thinking about the EVIL
> things which human nature wants. People who follow the Spirit
> are thinking about the things that the Spirit wants. The way
> human nature thinks is death, but the way the Spirit thinks is life
> and peace. The way human nature thinks is hatred for God.
> It doesn't want to put itself under the law of God. It can't! People
> controlled by human nature cannot please God.

However YOU are not being controlled by human nature; you are being controlled by the Spirit—if God's Spirit lives in you. If anyone does not have Christ's Spirit, this person does not belong to Christ. But since Christ is in you, even though your body is dying (because of sin), your spirit is alive (because you have been made right with God). And if the Spirit of the One who raised Jesus from death lives in you, then the One who raised Christ from death will make your dead bodies live, using the Spirit who is living in you.

Therefore, brothers, we shouldn't live by following our human nature. If you do, you will die. If you use the Spirit to kill the evil deeds of the body, you will live. All people who are being led by God's Spirit are sons of God. God did not give you a spirit to make you slaves, to be afraid again. Instead, you received THE Spirit WHO makes you sons. Through the Spirit, we cry out, "Father, dear Father!" This same spirit agrees with our spirits, that we are God's children. Since we are children, we are also heirs— heirs of God and co-heirs with Christ. If we suffer together, we will share glory together (Romans 8:5-16, SEB).

B. Have you ever dreamed that some day someone would knock on your door and hand you information showing that you have inherited a fortune from a forgotten relative? Dream no more! In obeying the gospel, you became a member of Christ's body, a **child of God!** No longer do you need to be afraid. Nothing outside yourself can separate you from God's loving care. You actually, in this life and in eternity, can enjoy, as joint heirs with Christ, God's wonderful gifts.

1. Just before his great challenge to a sacrificial life, Paul warns that the Jews were cut off because they did not believe, and that the same fate awaits Gentiles if they depart from their faith. A kind and loving God extends the opportunity for eternal salvation to all, but His strict justice demands that those who do not continue to obey must be cut off: "So you see that God is kind, but he can also be very strict. God punishes those people who stop following him. But God is kind to you, if you continue following his kindness. If you don't continue following him, you will be cut off *from the tree*" (Romans 11:22, ERV).

Behold, therefore, the goodness and severity of God!

2. The person who is not guilty has no reason to be afraid of an officer of the law. In the same way, as faithful children of God, we have no reason to be afraid of His strict justice. In this world, we can enjoy the rich rewards of a life devoted to Him and look forward to eternal life with God, Christ, and the Holy Spirit along with the saints of all ages:

41

*In the past you were slaves to sin, and goodness **(right living)** did not control you. You did evil things. Now you are ashamed of those things. Did those things help you? No. Those things only bring **spiritual** death. But now you are free from sin. You are now slaves of God. And this brings you a life that is only for God. And from that you will get life forever. When people sin, they earn what sin pays—death. But God gives his people a free gift— life forever in Christ Jesus our Lord (Romans 6:20-23, ERV).*

Conclusion: What a magnificent future awaits us as children of God! With all of Christendom, we can await with excitement for the time when God will "hand us our paycheck"—eternal life. I'm ready. Are you? Let's say to Paul, "We accept your challenge. We are ready to be **living sacrifices** for God! We join you in praise to our heavenly Father":

Yes, God's riches are very great! God's wisdom and knowledge have no end! No person can explain the things God decides. No person can understand God's ways. Like the Scripture says, "Who knows the mind of the Lord? Who is able to give God advice?" (Isaiah 40:13).

Who has ever given God anything? God owes nothing to any person (Job 41:11).

Yes, God made all things. And everything continues through God and for God. To God be the glory forever! Amen (Romans 11:33-36, ERV).

Daily Bible Reading

Sunday

*Righteousness by Faith in Practice
(Romans 6)*

Monday

*How To Be Free from the Law
(Romans 7)*

Tuesday

*Free from Condemnation,
Complication and Separation
(Romans 8)*

Wednesday

*God's Choice—To Fulfill His Purpose
(Romans 9)*

Thursday

*A Zeal for God Without Knowledge
(Romans 10)*

Friday

*The Goodness and Severity of God
(Romans 11)*

Saturday

*Alive in Christ
(Ephesians 2)*

Memory Verses

Matthew 6:33,34

Romans 6:22,23

Romans 8:37-39

Chapter 4

Your Life's Purpose

Introduction: Paul asked, after showing our need and God's grace to fill that need, that you and I present our bodies a **living sacrifice**. We are asked to present an offering—ourselves! God will not force us to do this. He loves a cheerful giver. The choice is ours. But of course we have made that choice when the Good News of the gospel touched our good and honest hearts. Christ became our life. With steadfast purpose, we dedicate our every thought, word, and deed to His glory. Like Barnabas, the man of encouragement, we share our purpose with others: "When he came and saw the grace of God, he was glad; and he exhorted them all to remain faithful to the Lord with steadfast purpose" (Acts 11:23, RSV).

I. Early Christian martyrs literally died for Christ. In most countries today, we are not in danger of physical death when we are truly living a Christian life. It is regrettable that, through the centuries, many battles have been fought between those purportedly following Christ, in the **name** of religion. What a tragedy this is when they are following traditions of men rather than learning from the New Testament what God's love has made possible through Christ.

Even animal sacrifices, under the old law, were brought to the altar alive; then they were slain by the priests and offered to God according to His ordinances. We learn that it was necessary for Christ to present Himself as the perfect sacrifice, which the prophets had foretold:

> *Those people's sacrifices make them remember their sins every year, because it is not possible for the blood of bulls and goats to take away sins. So when Christ came into the world he said: "You (GOD) don't want sacrifices and offerings, but you have prepared a body for me. You are not pleased with the sacrifices of animals killed and burned. And you are not pleased with sacrifices to take*

45

away sins. Then I said, 'Here I am, God. It is written about me in the book of the law. I have come to do the things you want' " (Psalm 40:6-8; Hebrews 10:3-7; ERV).

We have died—to sin—and are alive to Christ. You will remember that Paul made this so clear:

> *Since we died with Christ, we believe we will also live with him. You know that Christ was raised from death, never to die again— death does not rule over him anymore! This was the type of death he died: He died for sin, once for all time, but the kind of life he now lives is for God. In the same way think of yourselves as being dead to sin, but alive to God by Christ Jesus (Romans 6:8-11, SEB).*

A. What a glorious thought: no longer enslaved to sin! As our youngsters would say, "We'd better, then, clean up our act!" We noted that Satan may "beef up" his efforts to buy us back, offering all kinds of enticements. But the Holy Spirit, working in and for us, will help us battle sin. Christ is interceding for us. We will have the power to escape the domination of sin:

> *Therefore don't let sin rule over your dying bodies. Don't obey the desires of your bodies. Don't allow the members of your body to be used as evil tools for sin. Instead, give yourselves to God as people who have come back to life from death. Use the members of your body as righteous tools for God. Sin shall not rule over you, because you are not under the law—you are under God's gracious love! (Romans 6:12-14, SEB).*

1. God can and will help us to "mortify the flesh"—to kill the carnal desires, replacing them with spiritual purpose. Sometimes the Christian life is presented in such a way that people who have not heard the Word for themselves conclude that it is totally negative, simply made up of "thou shalt nots"! Repeatedly, we are told to remove from our lives things that would hinder our spiritual growth and influence. But in following passages, we are told what we are to add. The Christian life cannot be a vacuum. If we do not replace the sin that is removed with righteousness, we are in danger of dying spiritually, being worse off than we were before.

a. The sacrificial life is one of self-denial. As Jesus emptied Himself to take the likeness of man and to become obedient to death on the cross, He asks that we accept our share of the burden as we follow Him: "Then said Jesus unto his disciples, If any **man** will come after me, let him deny himself, and take up his cross,

46

and follow me. For whosoever will save his life shall lose it: and whosoever will lose his life for my sake shall find it. For what is a man profited, if he shall gain the whole world, and lose his own soul? or what shall a man give in exchange for his soul?" (Matthew 16:24-26, KJ).

b. If the whole world could not repay us for the loss of our souls, and if there is no way we could ever pay enough to buy back a soul facing God's just judgment unprepared, we have the very strongest motivation to destroy the carnal impulses that can fool us. Jesus warned that we must be continually ready, on the alert: "Be careful! Don't spend your time drinking and getting drunk. Or don't be too busy with worldly things. If you do that, you will not be able to think right. And then the end might come when you are not ready. It will come like a surprise to all people on earth. So be ready all the time. Pray that you will be strong enough to continue safely through all these things that will happen. And pray that you will be able to stand before the Son of Man" (Luke 21:34-36, ERV).

2. Many times, in writing to churches, Paul listed the works of the flesh, contrasting them with the fruit of the Spirit. The person whose life is dedicated to Christ will do all in her power to make a clean sweep of sin:

So put all evil things out of your life: sexual sinning, doing evil, letting evil thoughts control you, wanting things that are evil, and always selfishly wanting more and more. This wanting really means to live serving a false god. These things make God angry. In your evil life in the past, you also did these things.

But now put these things out of your life: anger, being very mad, doing or saying things to hurt other people, and using evil words when you talk. Don't lie to each other. Why? Because you have left your old sinful life and the things you did before. You have begun to live the new life (Colossians 3:5-10a, ERV).

3. Before identifying the works of the flesh, in writing to Galatian Christians, Paul urged a spiritual walk in order to win the battle with the flesh:

Brothers, although God called you to be free, don't use your freedom as an excuse to do all of the things which your physical body wants. Instead, serve each other through love. The entire law is made complete in this one command: "Love other people in the same way you love yourself" (Leviticus 19:18).

Be careful if you continue hurting each other and tearing each other apart, you might completely destroy one another!

So, I tell you: Live by following the Spirit. Then you won't do

the SELFISH and EVIL THINGS which you want in your human
nature. The human nature wants the things which are against the
Spirit. The Spirit wants things which are against our human
nature. These oppose each other. Because of this, you cannot do
*the things that you really intend to do. But if you let **the** Spirit lead*
*you, you are not under **the** law (Galatians 5:13-18, ERV).*

B. With the help of the Spirit, we will win the battle with our worldly nature and live a victorious life in Christ. If we have a little difficulty applying the scriptures to our lives, we should not be discouraged. Jesus told His apostles more than once who He was, His purpose in coming to the earth, that He would prepare a place for them and come back to claim them.

"You know the way," He said.

"We do not know where you are going, how can we know the way?" Thomas asked.

This prompted the Lord's wonderful assurance: "I am the way, the truth, and the life; no one comes to the father but by me" (John 14:6).

1. Jesus is **all** to the one who, through accepting the truth, has made up her mind to walk with Him in **the way**. This **is** life! John wrote, "This is what God told us: He has given us eternal life. This eternal life is in His Son. The person who has the Son has life, but the person who doesn't have the Son of God does not have life" (1 John 5:11,12, SEB).

2. Jesus came to give His followers abundant life. We need not be afraid of a deprived life, missing out on joy, happiness, and peace. Having rid ourselves of carnal desire, we will be ready for a life which is completely fulfilled. Perhaps the best known scripture in the whole Bible is Psalm 23 in which we, with David, claim the Lord as our shepherd. Jesus taught many lessons as He referred to Himself as the Good Shepherd who knows His sheep, walks and talks with them. We are the sheep whom He gives His loving care to afford us a life that is full and running over, far more than we had before. He assures us, "I came that they might have life, and that they might have it more abundantly" (John 10:10b, KJ).

C. How could we long for the old life, marred by sin, when we have such a wonderful promise of loving care? No, we are not promised that our path will have no thorns, but we are promised help in avoiding or getting rid of them. When the loving shepherd calls, his sheep listen and obey. They love him and prove it by doing what he says. In the same way, we show our love for Christ by hearing and obeying His Word (John 15:14). We deceive ourselves if we hear without responding. Obedience assures us a happy life: "But the truly happy person is the person who carefully studies God's teaching and does not forget what he heard. Then he obeys what God's teaching says. When that person does this, it makes that person happy" (James 1:25, ERV).

1. Some may think the Christian life restricts them from doing many desirable things. They may want to "sow their wild oats" before settling down to serve God. Many who have tried that route have learned to their sorrow that at least some of those things enslaved them. Actually, freedom is in Christ! Jesus told the.Pharisees that the truth would set them free. They were insulted, claiming they were descendants of Abraham and never had been slaves. Jesus answered them, "I am telling you the truth: every person who continues to sin is a slave of sin. A slave does not live in the house forever, but a son will always live there. If the son sets you free, you are truly free" (John 8:34-36, SEB).

2. Great things are promised the one who loses herself in Christ. She does not miss the self she crucified in order to let Christ live in her. Anticipating the glory she one day will share with Christ, she gladly fills her cleansed life with attitudes and actions becoming to the child of the King. Christ **is** her life:

> If then you have been raised with Christ, seek the things that are above, where Christ is, seated at the right hand of God. Set your minds on things that are above, not on things that are on earth. For you have died, and your life is hid with Christ in God. When Christ who is our life appears, then you also will appear with him in glory . . .
>
> Put on then, as God's chosen ones, holy and beloved, compassion, kindness, lowliness, meekness, and patience, forbearing one another and, if one has a complaint against another, forgiving each other; as the Lord has forgiven you, so you also must forgive. And above all these put on love, which binds everything together in perfect harmony. And let the peace of Christ rule in your hearts, to which you were called in the one body. And be thankful. Let the word of Christ dwell in you richly, as you teach and admonish one another in all wisdom, and as you sing psalms and hymns and spiritual songs with thankfulness in your hearts to God. And whatever you do, in word or deed, do everything in the name of the Lord Jesus, giving thanks to God the Father through him (Colossians 3:1-4,12-17, RSV).

II. A living sacrifice is **holy**. The one who had given herself to vice and wickedness, when cleansed by the blood of Christ, can give herself wholly to righteousness. Her purpose is to be really good, which sometimes is defined as suited to its purpose. Paul wrote, "As ye have yielded your members servants to uncleanness and to iniquity unto iniquity; even so now yield your members servants unto holiness . . . But now being made free from sin, and become servants to God, ye have your fruit unto holiness, and the end everlasting life" (Romans 6:19,22, KJ).

Holiness is the goal of one devoted to the Lord. She is on the alert for anything which would come between her and God. The writer of Hebrews admonishes, "Try to be at peace with everyone. Try to be holy. If you are not holy, you will never see the Lord" (Hebrews 12:14, SEB).

A. A Christian is a saint; she is sanctified; several writers use **sanctification** where others translate the same word **holiness**. It was understood under the old law that anything holy was set apart for the Lord's use. One who is sanctified is thus set apart, consecrated to the Lord.

1. Have you taken part in some game at school where two leaders chose the opposing players? Remember what a joy it was to be chosen, especially by someone you really liked. You felt honored, set apart. Then there were those who were always chosen last. Repeated often enough, this could kill their self-esteem. Now imagine that God is looking over those He can use. You might think He would choose the most capable. Of course, He uses people of varying abilities, but He can take the most inept and make him really useful:

Brothers ***and sisters****, God called (****chose****) you. Think about that! And not many of you were wise in the way the world judges wisdom. Not many of you had great influence. Not many of you came from important families. But God chose the foolish things of the world to give shame to the wise people. God chose the weak things of the world to give shame to the strong people. And God chose what the world thinks is not important. He chose what the world hates and thinks is nothing. God chose these to destroy what the world thinks is important. God did this so that no man can boast before him. It is God that has made you part of Christ Jesus. Christ has become wisdom for us from God. Christ is the reason we are holy and right with God, and have freedom (1 Corinthians 1:26-30, ERV).*

2. We must not get the impression that God has decided who will be saved and who will not—individually, that is. He wants everyone to be saved, but He is a just God. He stands ready always to save those who obey. Just how, then, did He call or choose us? Again, let's go to the scripture for answer: "But we are bound to give thanks to God always for you, brethren beloved by the Lord, because God chose you from the beginning to be saved, through sanctification by the Spirit and belief in the truth. To this he called you through our gospel, so that you may obtain the glory of our Lord Jesus Christ" (2 Thessalonians 2:13,14, RSV).

Another translation says, "He called you by using the Good News that we preached" (ERV). We learned that the call of the gospel is to every nation, every creature. He chooses those who obey!

B. Thus, a person who is holy is in the right relationship with God. You are a new creation with a new personality or nature. It is the very best, for it is "created after the likeness of God in true righteousness and holiness" (Ephesians 4:24, RSV).

Since God is love, you are, above all, a loving person. You love not only those who love you, but even those who hate you. You love the unlovely. Certainly, the love for family differs from the concern for those who need us, but God's love extends to them through us. John wrote, "And so we know the love that God has for us, and we trust that love. God is love. The person who lives in love lives in God. And God lives in that person. If God's love is made perfect in us, then we can be without fear on the day when God judges us. We will be without fear, because in this world we are like him *(Christ or God)"* (1 John 4:16,17, ERV).

C. The person who is sanctified—set apart for God's use— lives a life suited for sacred use. Not only does this kind of life meet God's approval, but it demands the respect of outsiders. They may be led to a right relationship with God by your example:

> God wants you to be holy. He wants you to stay away from sexual sins. God wants each one of you to learn to control your own body. Use your body in a way that is holy and that gives honor to God . . . None of you should do wrong to your brother **in Christ** or cheat him in this way. The Lord will punish people that do those things. We have already told you and warned you about that. God called us to be holy. He does not want us to live in sin. So the person who refuses to obey this teaching is refusing to obey God, not man. And God is the One who gives us his Holy Spirit . . . Do all you can to live a peaceful life. Take care of your own business. Do your own work. We have already told you to do these things. If you do these things, then people who are not believers will respect the way you live. And you will not have to depend on other people for what you need (1 Thessalonians 4:3,4,6-8,11,12, ERV).

III. Any sacrifice to God must be acceptable, pleasing to Him. Sacrifices were a great part of the ceremonial law in the Mosaic Age. Not every offering was acceptable. The wrong kind of animal or an acceptable animal brought with the wrong motive or life out of keeping with God's ordinances made those sacrifices an abomination to God. Speaking to the Pharisees, Jesus said, "Ye are they which justify yourselves before men; but God knoweth your hearts: for that which is highly esteemed among men is abomination in the sight of God" (Luke 16:15, KJ).

A. King Saul gives us a vivid example of partial obedience, which made his sacrifices unacceptable and cost him his kingdom. God had commanded him to wipe out the Amalekites completely—people, livestock, everything. God sent Samuel to confront Saul, and the king declared that he had fulfilled his assignment. When the prophet called his attention to the cattle and spoils of war he had brought back, he replied, "I brought back King Agag, and the people brought the finest animals to sacrifice to God." And Samuel said:

> *Has the Lord as much delight in burnt offerings and sacrifices as in obeying the voice of the Lord? Behold, to obey is better than sacrifice, and to heed than the fat of rams. For rebellion is as the sin of divination, and insubordination is as iniquity and idolatry. Because you have rejected the word of the Lord, He has also rejected you from being king (1 Samuel 15:22,23, NASV).*

B. The Pharisees of Jesus' day were very conscientious in their giving of tithes, but Jesus gave them a scathing rebuke for their failure in interpersonal matters: "Woe to you, scribes and Pharisees, hypocrites! for you tithe mint and dill and cummin, and have neglected the weightier matters of the law, justice and mercy and faith; these you ought to have done, without neglecting the others. You blind guides, straining out a gnat and swallowing a camel!" (Matthew 23:23,24, RSV).

C. We may, because of duty or fear of punishment, go through the motions of dedication to the Lord. But if we are not motivated by love, we gain nothing:

> *I may speak in different languages of men or even angels. But if I don't have love, then I am only a noisy bell or a ringing cymbal. I may have the gift of prophecy; I may understand all the secret things **of God** and all knowledge; and I may have faith so great that I can move mountains. But even with all these things, if I don't have love then I am nothing. I may give my body **as an***

offering *to be burned. But I gain nothing by doing these things if I don't have love (1 Corinthians 13:1-3, ERV).*

IV. With pure heart and action in keeping with our purpose, we can offer ourselves as a living sacrifice, pleasing to God.

A. Jesus Christ is our example. Although He was, and is, the Son of God, He never presumed to put His will above the Father's. In fact, His purpose was to do the Father's will: "I came down from heaven to do what God wants me to do. I did not come to do what I want to do" (John 6:38, ERV).

Jesus had walked purposefully toward the cross, even when His apostles protested, but the flesh wrestled with the spirit as He prayed in the garden. In agony he cried, "Father, if thou be willing, remove this cup from me: nevertheless, not my will, but thine, be done" (Luke 22:42, KJ).

B. Our offering is acceptable when we do good and are willing to share our lives and our possessions.

1. God expects us to be good citizens. Although Jesus may have been considered a revolutionary, he did not attempt to change governments. His mission was to change people. When asked about paying taxes, He replied, "Render to God the things that are God's and to Caesar the things that are Caesar's." Paul gave instruction that we are to be subject to the governing powers: "For rulers are not a terror to good conduct, but to bad. Would you have no fear of him who is in authority? Then do what is good, and you will receive his approval" (Romans 13:3, RSV).

2. He expects us, first, to be good women, to glorify Him in whatever we do. For those of us who choose to marry and rear a family, He expects us to be good wives, mothers, and even in-laws. Several New Testament scriptures define our roles. Whether we are Christian career women or homemakers, or both, if we do a good job, our bodies are living sacrifices, pleasing to God! You probably are familiar with Titus 2:3-5, but let's look at it again, briefly:

Also teach the older women to be holy in the way they live. Teach them not to speak against other people, or to have the habit of drinking too much wine. Those women should teach what is good. In that way they can teach the younger women to love their husbands and children. They can teach the younger women to be wise and to be pure, to take care of their homes, to be kind, and to obey their husbands. Then no person will be able to criticize the teaching God gave us (ERV).

53

Also, in 1 Timothy, the fifth chapter, Paul gives some valuable instruction on family relationships and the things that are expected of us as women. He indicates that women who have lived good lives may be supported by the church, but he declares that children and grandchildren should be responsible for care of the elderly. A beautiful example of that teaching in action may be seen in the family of Belle Case here in Tulsa. She is in her nineties, but she has never failed to have the loving care of one of her three daughters or her son and his wife. In fact, each of the family members receives the same ministry by the brothers and sisters, all of whom now are of retirement age.

V. Paul concludes his plea for a sacrificial life by describing it as "your reasonable service" (KJ), "your spiritual service" (RSV), "your spiritual service" (ASV), "your spiritual service of worship" (NASV), and "the worship offered by mind and heart" (NEB).

To me, the King James Version had always been somewhat comforting. If God expected the product of my sacrificial life to be just "reasonable" service, I might rationalize myself into doing about as I pleased. But to include my whole life as spiritual worship shed a whole new light on the subject. If worship is paying due homage, then we can glorify God by doing a good job of washing dishes, for remember, we are to teach the younger women to care for their homes!

A. Paul asked that our bodies be a living sacrifice. I learn from Paul, again, that my body is a temple! We may think our generation invented sexual sin, but not so! Again and again, Paul warns against it, exclaiming in one of the epistles, "Surely you realize that your bodies are parts of Christ's body . . . Run away from sexual sin! Any other sin which a person might do is outside his body, but if a person commits a sexual sin, he is sinning against his own body. Surely you realize that your body is a temple sanctuary? You have received the Holy Spirit from God. The Holy Spirit is inside you—in the temple sanctuary. You don't belong to yourselves. You were bought; you cost something. Use your bodies to give glory to God" (1 Corinthians 6:15,18-20, SEB).

B. We are to offer the sacrifice of praise, which certainly can be done in individual or corporate worship. We read, "So through Jesus we should never stop offering our sacrifice to God. That sacrifice is our praise, coming from lips that speak his name. And don't forget to do good for other people. These are the sacrifices that please God" (Hebrews 13:15,16, ERV).

C. Under the Law of Moses, sacrifices always were offered by priests. Christians are priests under the new law. Yes—you, a woman, **are** a priest in that you can go directly to God through our High Priest, Jesus Christ. You certainly can offer your body a living sacrifice, acceptable to God!

We have purified our bodies through obedience to the truth:

So put away all malice and all guile and insincerity and envy and all slander. Like newborn babes, long for the pure spiritual milk, that by it you may grow up to salvation; for you have tasted the kindness of the Lord.

Come to him, to that living stone, rejected by men but in God's sight chosen and precious; and like living stones be yourselves built into a spiritual house, to be a holy priesthood, to offer spiritual sacrifices acceptable to God through Jesus Christ (1 Peter 2:1-5, RSV).

Daily Bible Reading

Sunday

Christ, Our Sacrifice
(Hebrews 10)

Monday

Christ Is Your Life!
(Colossians 3)

Tuesday

The Conflict of Carnal and Spiritual
(Galatians 5)

Wednesday

A Place for You
(John 14)

Thursday

Obedience Leads to Happiness
(James 1)

Friday

God Is Love
(1 John 4)

Saturday

God Wants You to Be Holy
(1 Thessalonians 4)

Memory Verses

1 Peter 1:22-2:5

Chapter 5

Resist That Squeeze

Introduction: She was the loving matriarch of an area-wide group of professional and would-be writers. She was a spinster schoolteacher and writer who had become a popular radio personality. The writers were her "children." She always came directly to the point when she had something to write or say. Seeing a regional correspondent's byline on a story she liked, she penned a note: "I am to retire soon as president of Panhandle Pen Women. I want you to be a member before I step down. I am enclosing a copy of our bylaws."

So! They weren't just a group of old ladies talking about writing! One had to be a selling writer to maintain active membership. The novice accepted the invitation. Since she had difficulty saying "No!", she progressed eventually to the group's presidency.

Another letter from Laura demanded, "Let's do something about this!" Enclosed was a heart-rending appeal from an older member asking that the writers get her out of the nursing home she loathed.

Forgetting that she was younger and had less tenure than the matriarch, the president replied, "No! We can't do it! We were organized for **one purpose**—to encourage new women writers. If the woman has children, they are responsible for her. If not, other relatives or her church should see to her needs."

Relieving the distressed certainly was a good work, but in this case it was **outside the purpose** of the writer's group. We must never forget that **a living sacrifice** is **a purposeful life**! We must resist anything that would destroy its purpose. Anything the world does to try to "squeeze us into its mold" must be resisted. It may have to include also some things good in themselves which would dilute the effectiveness of our dedication to Christ. Our purpose is strengthened as we recall Paul's plea:

So brothers, with God's tender feelings, I beg you to offer your bodies as a living, holy, pleasing sacrifice to God. This is true wor-

57

ship from you. Don't act like people of this world. Instead, be changed inside by letting your mind be made new again. Then you can determine what is good, pleasing, and perfect—what God wants (Romans 12:1,2 SEB).

I. God has not promised that the Christian life will be easy. Jesus, in His prayer just before His crucifixion, asked not that His disciples be taken out of the world, but that they should be protected from the evil one (John 17:15). In fact, He sent them into all the world. Just as He had been tempted, He knew they would have to meet and overcome temptation.

A. We may not always recognize temptation. It is defined as that which leads or endeavors to lead into evil or undesirable action. It may try to entice us to do wrong by promises of pleasure or gain.

B. Satan is the temptor. Jesus recognized that he might present himself in various forms, even at times as servants of light. When Peter tried to divert Him from His purpose in going to the cross, Jesus said, "Get thee behind me, Satan" (Matthew 16:23b, KJ).

When urging the Corinthians to forgive and show their love to a penitent sinner, Paul reminded them that they should forgive the brother so that he would not give up completely: "I did this so that Satan (the devil) would not win anything from us. We know very well what Satan's plans are" (2 Corinthians 2:11, ERV). Satan uses many devices.

1. He appealed to Adam and Eve through the eye, the appetite, and the wisdom that would make them like gods:

> Now the serpent was more subtle than any other wild creature that the Lord God had made. He said to the woman, "Did God say, 'You shall not eat of any tree of the garden'?"
>
> And the woman said to the serpent, "We may eat of the fruit of the trees of the garden; but God said, 'You shall not eat of the fruit of the tree which is in the midst of the garden, neither shall you touch it, lest you die.' "
>
> But the serpent said to the woman, "You will not die. For God knows that when you eat of it your eyes will be opened, and you will be like God, knowing good and evil."
>
> So when the woman saw that the tree was good for food, and that it was a delight to the eyes, and that the tree was to be desired to make one wise, she took of its fruit and ate; and she also gave some to her husband, and he ate (Genesis 3:1-7, RSV).

58

2. Satan really got off to a good start! We know that God placed a curse on him, and Jesus denounced those who followed him: "You are of your father the devil, and your will is to do your father's desires. He was a murderer from the beginning, and has nothing to do with the truth, because there is no truth in him. When he lies, he speaks according to his own nature, for he is a liar and the father of lies" (John 8:44, RSV).

3. Satan is as near to the truth as light is to dark. His delight is to blind others to the truth: "We don't use trickery, and we don't change the teaching of God. No! But we teach the truth plainly. This is how we show people who we are. And this is how they can know in their hearts what kind of people we are before God. The Good News that we preach may be hidden. But it is hidden only to those people who are lost. The ruler of this world *(the devil)* has blinded the minds of people who don't believe. They cannot see the light *(truth)* of the Good News—the Good News about the glory of Christ" (2 Corinthians 4:2b-4b, ERV).

4. He tried the same tricks on Jesus that he used on Eve (Matthew 4:1-11).

C. Jesus Christ died to overcome sin, but He did not chain the devil. Satan still is subtle, and he tries his whole bag of tricks on people today. He looks for our weakest points and makes his attack there. It seems at times that he redoubles his efforts on new Christians, determined to regain those he has lost to Christ. He can make his offers just as attractive now as he did in the Garden of Eden.

1. Solomon gave a very good example of his tactics, picturing very clearly the appeal to be one of the gang, be popular, get rich:

My son, if sinners entice you, Do not consent. If they say, Come with us, Let us lie in wait for blood; Let us wantonly ambush the innocent; Like Sheol let us swallow them alive and whole, Like those who go down to the pit; We shall find all precious goods; We shall fill our houses with spoil; Throw in your lot among us; We will all have one purse (Proverbs 1:10-14, RSV).

2. He also draws a vivid picture of the relentless nature of their enticement:

Do not walk in the way of evil men. Avoid it; do not go on it; Turn away from it, and pass on. For they cannot sleep unless they have done wrong; They are robbed of sleep unless they have made someone stumble. For they eat the bread of wickedness, and drink the wine of violence. But the path of the righteous is like *the light of dawn, Which shines brighter and brighter until full day. The way of the wicked is like deep darkness: They do not know over what they stumble (Proverbs 4:14b-19, RSV).*

D. Perhaps we are more easily led by rationalization than by the outright invitation to do wrong. We can rationalize just as Eve did! We may get into what is called "grey areas," where it may be difficult to distinguish between wrong and right. Wrong may be presented as an alternative, an acceptable way of life.

1. Every mother or father has heard the pitiful plea, "Everybody's doing it!" The children next door may be allowed to do things we feel will work against their Christian influence. It may be hard, but we must show our children that we're not "everybody's" parents. We are Christians and, in their parlance, walk "to the beat of a different drum."

2. We live in a country where, at least in theory, the majority rules. We listen to the news or see a television program almost every day where we see or hear people doing things that would not have been allowed on the media a few years ago. Going to bed with one after another of the opposite sex and living with someone to whom we are not married appear so often in televised or printed stories that they have become accepted as alternate life styles! These things are included in Paul's listing of the things that make God angry, concluding: "They know that God's law says that people who live like this should die. But they continue to do these wrong things. And they feel that people who do these things are doing right" (Romans 1:32, ERV).

3. Jesus told of two ways—one traveled by the majority, the other by only a few. He counseled, "Go through the narrow door *which leads to eternal life.* The door is wide and the road is broad which leads to destruction. Many people are entering through it. The door is small which leads to life and the road is narrow. Only a few people are finding it" (Matthew 7:13,14, ERB). Certainly, a thing **can** be wrong when the majority is doing it!

4. You might think I'm meddling if I list a few things which may hurt our effectiveness as Christians. So be it! We see a young woman wearing almost literally a few threads of clothing, or clothing which might cause a young man's mind to wander to thoughts which could condemn him, and we're told, "Everybody's wearing it!" We're offered an intoxicant or a harmful drug, and we get the same answer, or perhaps, "Just a little won't hurt!" Perhaps one of the most prevalent practices which may lead to ruin is gambling. Now it, along with alcoholism, is being classified as an ailment, which it might very well be; it is addictive.

5. Good can be made so attractive to our young people that they will want to do right. We know that those who are tempted are helped to resist by God's power working within us. We need not think, though, that we are too good or strong to yield to temptation. A man or woman may begin reading a pornographic magazine with the excuse that he needs to know what the world is reading. He may find himself reading more and more but finally, in disgust, he throws it away and turns back to God's Word for strength. We are promised, "The person who thinks he is safe should be careful—he might fall! You have been tempted the same way all people have been tempted, but God is faithful. He will not allow *Satan* to tempt you with more than you can resist. No, when you are being tempted, God will also give you a way to escape, so that you can endure it" (1 Corinthians 10:12,13, SEB).

We must learn to use the weapon Jesus used when Satan tempted Him:

> *Jesus returned from the Jordan River. He was full of the Holy Spirit. The Spirit led Jesus into the desert. There the devil tempted Jesus for 40 days. Jesus ate nothing during that time. When those days were finished, Jesus was very hungry.*
>
> *The devil said to Jesus, "If you are the Son of God, tell this rock to become bread."*
>
> *Jesus answered, "It is written in the Scriptures: 'A person does not live only by eating food' " (Deuteronomy 8:3).*
>
> *Then the devil took Jesus and showed him all the kingdoms of the world in a moment of time. The devil said to Jesus, "I will give you all these kingdoms and all the power and glory that is in them. It has all been given to me. I can give it to any person I want. I will give it all to you, if you will only worship me."*
>
> *Jesus answered, "It is written in the Scriptures: 'You must worship the Lord your God; Serve only him!' " (Deuteronomy 6:13).*
>
> *Then the devil led Jesus to Jerusalem. The devil put Jesus on a very high place of the temple. He said to Jesus, "If you are the Son of God, jump off! It is written in the Scriptures: 'God will command his angels to take care of you' (Psalm 91:11). It is also written: 'Their hands will catch you so that you will not hit your foot on a rock' " (Psalm 91:12).*
>
> *Jesus answered. "But it also says in the Scriptures: 'You must not test (**doubt**) the Lord your God" (Deuteronomy 6:16) — Luke 4:1-13, ERV.*

II. The flesh in which we live can be very demanding. We can be tempted as Jesus was by the lust of the flesh. Of course, He met that temptation head-on and overcame it. We can meet the impulses and imaginations of our evil natures in the same way. We must always be alert; Satan stays on the job.

A. Paul begins his catalogue of the works of the flesh with sexual sins: adultery, fornication, uncleanness, lasciviousness. These are, primarily, sins of passion (Galatians 5:19).

1. Adultery is defined as having unlawful intercourse with the spouse of another. Both parties in a wedding ceremony promise to keep themselves unto this one partner alone. They break that vow when they commit adultery. This cannot be passed off lightly as "a little affair." It can, however, be forgiven. Remember, Jesus said to the woman taken in adultery, "Go and sin no more" (John 8:11, KJ).

2. Fornication is described as **illicit** sexual intercourse. This would not entail breaking of the marriage troth, as in adultery; it simply means **anyone** who does not have God's approval of such intimacy. Paul indicated that each person should have a spouse to fulfill the natural and wholesome desires we were given to encourage love and procreation. He did say, however, it is good for a person who can control his desire to live a celibate life, devoting himself to the Lord. He adds that it is not a sin to marry and recognizes marriage as necessary for some: "But if they cannot control their bodies, they should marry. It is better to marry than to burn with sexual desire" (1 Corinthians 7:9, ERV). Today's **alternate life style**—living without marriage—is condemned.

3. In current translations, another popular "life style" of which we never heard a generation ago—at least above a whisper—is also condemned. Some are equating the rights of homosexuals with those of citizens of different races. Remember the old rule? Things equal to the same things are equal to each other. The scriptures make it clear that people of all nations have access to salvation through the gospel, under Christ. They make it just as clear that homosexuality is a sin, catalogued with what we consider to be the vilest: "Women stopped having natural sex with men. They started having sex with other women. In the same way, men stopped having natural sex with women. The men began wanting each other all the time. Men did shameful things with other men. And in their bodies they received the punishment for those wrong things they did" (Romans 1:26b-27, ERV).

4. As I am writing this, thousands are marching in Washington to protest the legalization of abortion by the Supreme Court. Pro-abortionists contend that a woman should have the right to her own body, to say whether she would give birth to the child in her womb or have it killed. We are told that children are a gift from God (Psalm 127:3), and that of such is the kingdom of heaven (Mark

10:14). Some contend that the **fetus** is not a human being with rights of its own until it breathes, lives independently. We are told that God gives **life** and **breath** (Acts 17:25). Why would each have been named if there were not life without breath? Indeed, a fetus which is not alive will be aborted spontaneously.

Jesus endorsed, by telling a young man to keep the commandments, the forbidding of taking human life: "Thou shalt do no murder" (Matthew 19:18, KJ). Literature is available indicating that even those who do not suffer guilt because of religious beliefs undergo psychological trauma after an abortion.

B. We cannot ignore the remainder of the works of the flesh listed by Paul: idolatry, sorcery, enmity, strife, jealousy, anger, selfishness, dissension, party spirit, envy, drunkenness, carousing, and the like (Galatians 5:19-21, RSV). That same scripture warns that those who do such things shall not inherit the kingdom of God. Some of these we have discussed previously, and they can have just as devastating effect on the Christian life as the sexual sins. Our society tends, also, to condone at least some of them.

It is encouraging that some of the rebellion, the "do your own thing" spirit of the 1960s, is passing; our college students have become serious in the pursuit of an education. Certainly one who is **a living sacrifice** cannot be selfish! Remember, Jesus said we must lose self if we would be His disciple. Paul considered himself crucified for Christ but living, with Christ living in him.

III. Satan tried to tempt Jesus by offering Him everything. We can succumb to the temptation of wanting "everything your little heart desires." A part of the student rebellion was against materialism, perhaps rightly so. Jesus said, you know, that life is more than owning **things** (Luke 12:15). Having as our purpose in life the acquisition of wealth is at cross purposes with a life dedicated to Christ. Jesus said, "You cannot serve God and money *at the same time*" (Luke 16:13, SEB).

A. Actually, the things we say we own really belong to God; we are simply given them as His stewards. The Psalmist said, "The earth is the Lord's and the fulness thereof, the world and those who dwell therein" (Psalm 24:1, RSV). David pointed out that what we gave to God really belonged to Him: "But who am I, and what is my people, that we should be able thus to offer willingly? For all things come from thee, and of thy own have we given thee" (1 Chronicles 29:14, RSV).

B. When we hear the little "beep" heralding a weather warning to be given on television, we pay close attention, especially if we are planning a trip. As we live a surrendered life, we are traveling from earth to heaven. Jesus warned against all covetousness, translated "greed" and even "selfishness" in some versions. He was asked to arbitrate between two brothers who were quarreling over their inheritance when He said, "Be careful and guard against all kinds of greed. A person's life is not measured by the things he owns" (Luke 12:15, SEB).

He then used the parable of the farmer who had to build new barns to store his bountiful crop. He thought he had it made, saying, "I have many good things stored. I have saved enough for many years. Relax, eat, drink, celebrate!"

But God said to that man, "Foolish man! Tonight you will die. So, what about the things you prepared? Who will own those things now?" (Luke 12:19b,20, SEB).

People commit all kinds of sins for money. Women and girls are driven to prostitution. Men steal and kill. Jezebel had Naboth killed because Ahab coveted Naboth's vineyard (1 Kings 21:1-19).

Those whose purpose is to get rich are skating on the edge of disaster. Paul sums it up by pointing out true riches contrasted with the material:

> It is true that serving God makes a person very rich, if that person is satisfied with what he has. When we came into the world, we brought nothing. And when we die, we can take nothing out. So, if we have food and clothes, we will be satisfied with that. People who want to become rich bring temptations to themselves. They are caught in a trap. They begin to want many foolish things that will hurt them. Those things ruin and destroy people. The love of money causes all kinds of evil. Some people have left the TRUE faith (TEACHING) because they want to get more and more money. But they have caused themselves to be very, very sad (1 Timothy 6:6-10, ERV).

IV. When Satan asked Jesus to jump from the pinnacle of the temple, the Son of God used scripture to show why He refused to tempt God—that is, to put God to the test, to see if He would do what He said He would. He did not succomb to the "pride of life." It was not in His nature to boast, to "show off."

Vainglory is described as "excessive pride in one's performance." We are warned, "Let nothing be done through strife or vainglory; but in lowliness of mind let each esteem other better than themselves" (Philippians 2:3, KJ). Other translations use "selfishness or conceit" (RSV) and "rivalry and personal vanity" (NEB). In verses following the above quotation, we are told to let Christ's mind be in us, let our attitude be like His. He did not cling to equality with God but chose to be confined in a human body, to become the perfect sacrifice for our sins.

Conclusion: One who has the mind of Christ will not adapt herself to the pattern of this present world. With the sword of the Spirit, she will ward off the lust of the flesh, the lust of the eye, and the pride of life, just as Jesus did.

Daily Bible Reading

Sunday
A Sacrificial Life
(Romans 12)

Monday
From Paradise to Poverty
(Genesis 3)

Tuesday
Don't Trust Sinners!
(Proverbs 1:10-14; 4:4-19)

Wednesday
Use That Sword!
(Matthew 4:1-11; Luke 4:1-13)

Thursday
The Spiritual Battle
(Galatians 5)

Friday
Use Riches Properly—
Don't Let Them Rule You!
(1 Timothy 6)

Saturday
Have the Mind of Christ!
(Philippians 2:1-18)

Memory Verses

Matthew 7:13,14
1 John 2:15,16

Chapter 6

Use God's Transformer

Introduction: Why does your electrician install a transformer? It is because the voltage must be changed to supply the **power** required by your new appliance. As you present your body a living sacrifice in primary obedience and continue to grow toward the likeness of Christ, you can no longer get your power from the world or things in it. God's transformer provides the **power** to make your minds and hearts new again. In this way, His power can work through you. You undergo a metamorphosis. Your old life resembled a lowly cocoon. Your new life soars like a beautiful butterfly . . . an eagle!

This, actually, is the process through which we become and remain a living sacrifice:

> *Therefore, my brethren, I implore you by God's mercy to offer your very selves to him: a living sacrifice, dedicated and fit for his acceptance, the worship offered by mind and heart. Adapt yourselves no longer to the pattern of this present world, but let your minds be remade and your whole nature thus transformed. Then you will be able to discern the will of God, and to know what is good, acceptable, and perfect (Romans 12:1,2, NEB).*

I. Many people have been reared in a moral atmosphere. They may not think their minds need to be remade; certainly, they do not have the obstacles to overcome that one does whose whole environment is corrupt or tends in that direction. Just this week, I heard of a girl in junior high who was constantly embarrassed because of the filthy language pouring from the mouths of her seat mates. She needs the help of the Spirit, supplying God's power, to sweep that filth from her mind and keep her from bitterness. They need a complete spiritual overhaul! Her mind needs renewal, made new again; theirs need to be remade, changed completely.

A. God can take the most reprobate mind and make it fit for His use. The psalmist David recognized his need and sought God's favor:

> Purge me with hyssop, and I shall be clean: wash me, and I shall be whiter than snow . . . Hide thy face from my sins, and blot out all my iniquities. Create in me a clean heart, O God; and put a new and right spirit within me (Psalm 51:7,9,10, RSV).

1. The carnal mind needs a thorough cleansing. God just cannot stand it. One whose mind is corrupt is an enemy of God:

> People who follow human nature are thinking about the evil things which human nature wants. People who follow the Spirit are thinking about the things the Spirit wants. The way human nature thinks is death, but the way the Spirit thinks is life and peace. The way human nature thinks is hatred for God. It doesn't want to put itself under the law of God. It can't! People controlled by human nature cannot please God (Romans 8:5-8, SEB).

2. People with corrupt minds are useless to God; they are sick spiritually. They may pretend to know God, but their behavior betrays their real nature. They are frauds! Paul warned Titus about such people: "To the pure all things are pure, but to the corrupt and unbelieving nothing is pure; their very minds and consciences are corrupted. They profess to know God, but they deny him by their deeds; they are detestable, disobedient, unfit for any good deed" (Titus 1:15,16, RSV).

Notice that their consciences are corrupted. Like Paul before his conversion, they may in good conscience do things that are wrong. By the world, they have been led to think wrong is right. When a scripture disagrees with what we want to do, we might say, "But I feel in my heart this is all right." God's Word, not our feelings, will judge us. We need our conscience renewed!

3. If you choose to follow your human nature—your conscience—rather than God, that is contrary to His will, but He will let the decision be yours. Remember how Paul pictured the base nature of those who ignored all the evidence of God's existence and loving concern: "And since they did not see fit to acknowledge God, God gave them up to a base mind and to improper conduct. They were filled with all manner of wickedness" (Romans 1:28,29a, RSV).

4. The world may intrude on a mind and heart which is morally right but has not yielded itself wholly to God's direction.

They may hear and understand what they should do, but temporal concerns keep them from applying the teaching to their lives. In explaining the parable of the sower, Jesus said, "And what is the seed that fell among the thorny weeds? That seed is like the person who hears the teaching but lets worries about this life and love for money stop that teaching from growing. So that teaching does not make fruit in that person's life" (Matthew 13:22, ERV).

B. A merciful heavenly Father takes people who are in error because they are deceived, and even those who are hateful and rebellious, and makes them pure through a rebirth and endows them with the Holy Spirit to help them overcome their weaknesses. In his instruction to the young preacher, Titus, Paul wrote:

> For we ourselves were once foolish, disobedient, led astray, slaves to various passions and pleasures, passing our days in malice and envy, hated by men and hating one another; but when the goodness and loving kindness of God our Savior appeared, he saved us, not because of deeds done by us in righteousness, but in virtue of his own mercy, by the washing of regeneration and renewal in the Holy Spirit, which he poured out upon us richly through Jesus Christ our Savior (Titus 3:3-6a, RSV).

1. God's Word, inspired by the Spirit, is the transformer used to impart God's will to us, thus allowing obedient disciples to use the power available from heaven. Electricity may be coming through a transformer to an appliance, but nothing happens until we turn the switch. The same is true of God's Word; we may hear, read, or even memorize it, but we are just fooling ourselves if we do not turn it into action in our lives. Since a bit of trash may keep the power from being conveyed, the connections must be kept clean. Again and again, we are reminded that we have to cleanse our minds of prejudice so that the true word can work in us:

> Know this, my beloved brethren, Let every man be quick to hear, slow to speak, slow to anger, for the anger of man does not work the righteousness of God. Therefore put away all filthiness and rank growth of wickedness and receive with meekness the implanted word, which is able to save your souls. But be doers of the word, and not hearers only, deceiving yourselves (James 1:19-22, RSV).

My husband and I were forced to call AAA the other day when our car failed to start when we were away from home. The genial mechanic knew just what to do after hearing my husband's evaluation of the situation. He took a small tool and cleaned the battery post. Corrosion had made it impossible for the power to get through!

2. God's Word, used properly, is the tool which purifies the soul. Peter makes this very clear: "Having purified your souls by your obedience to the truth for a sincere love of the brethren, love one another earnestly from the heart. You have been born anew, not of perishable seed but of imperishable, through the living and abiding word of God" (1 Peter 1:22,23, RSV). The word is not a dead letter. It is living! Although attempts have been made to keep those words from the common people, they are available in more languages today than ever before. There are countries where people risk their lives to take the Word to those who are hungering and thirsting for its truth. May those of us who have such ready access to this life-giving message use and share it!

3. God has promised that His Word will do what He has planned for it to do. It was powerful when conveyed to the Israelites by the prophets. Many did not heed, but a remnant cleansed itself from idolatry from among the heathen nations. They returned to Jerusalem, never devoting themselves to idols again. Through them Jesus came, fulfilling Isaiah's message from God that the Word would accomplish its purpose:

> Seek the Lord while he may be found, call upon him while he is near; let the wicked forsake his way, and the unrighteous man his thoughts; let him return to the Lord, that he may have mercy on him, and to our God, for he will abundantly pardon. For my thoughts are not your thoughts, neither are your ways my ways, says the Lord. For as the heavens are higher than the earth, so are my ways higher than your ways and my thoughts higher than your thoughts.

> For the rain and the snow come down from heaven, and return not thither but water the earth, making it bring forth and sprout, giving seed to the sower and bread to the eater, so shall my word be that goes forth from my mouth; it shall not return to me empty, but it shall accomplish that which I purpose, and prosper in the thing for which I sent it (Isaiah 55:6-11, RSV).

C. So long as we are in touch with God's transformer, our spiritual lives are being renewed constantly. We are told our bodies are dying a little every day—at least we know that the popular saying is true: "This is the first day of the rest of your life." Paul reminded the Corinthians of the certainty that God raised Jesus from death and that He will raise the faithful to be with Jesus. This and God's continuing kindness bring more and more people to Christ and give assurance to the believers:

> This is why we never become weak. Our physical body is becoming older and weaker, but our spirit inside us is made new every day. We have small troubles for a while now, but those troubles are helping us gain an eternal glory. That eternal glory is much greater than the troubles. So we think about the things we cannot see, not what we see. The things we see continue only a short time. And the things we cannot see will continue forever (2 Corinthians 4:16-18, ERV).

Jesus taught that spiritual life is transmitted through His teaching. Remember that Peter has urged that we have a very strong desire for the Word, which will last forever, in order that we may grow spiritually (1 Peter 2:2). He had been with Jesus and was convinced of the power of our Lord's message to us: "The Spirit is life-giving; physical things are not worth very much. The words I have spoken to you are Spirit and life" (John 6:63, SEB).

     1. As the Word is applied to our lives, we can escape anxiety and our hearts and minds will be at peace. Our thoughts will be in keeping with Christ's teaching; so the world will hinder our spiritual progress less and less. We will feel free to go to God with every request, assured that He cares and hears:

> The Lord is near. Don't worry about anything. Instead, let God know what you are asking for in prayer. Tell Him all about what you want. And, be thankful. God's peace, which goes far beyond all **human** understanding, will guard your hearts and minds in Christ Jesus.
>
> Finally, brothers, think about good things and things that will bring praise—whatever is true, noble, right, pure, lovely, and honorable. Practice the things you learned from me, received from me, heard from me, or saw in me. The God of peace will be with you (Philippians 4:5b-9, SEB).

How can we miss our spiritual goals when we have the example of Paul's life and teaching and the assurance that God Himself will keep our hearts and minds?

     2. Earlier in this wonderful letter to the Philippians, Paul urged Christians, "Let this mind be in you, which was also in Christ Jesus" (Philippians 2:5, KJ). Of course, we cannot have the physical mind of the Son of God, but we can shape our attitudes by His teaching. We can follow His example. We can imitate the humility which

71

caused Him to strip Himself of equality with God and the glories of heaven to live in a human body with its temptations and limitations. He claimed no glory for Himself, but glorified His Father in His teaching and actions. He fought the weakness of the flesh in the Garden of Gethsemane, yet yielded to His Father's eternal plan in His death on the cross. We can be obedient as He was obedient.

II. We have numerous examples in the New Testament of lives changed by Jesus. He chose to change the world by changing people. Even His apostles had trouble in realizing that His purpose was not to set up an earthly kingdom but a spiritual one, composed of those cleansed from sin and added to His body, the church.

Most of us can identify with Peter, whom someone has referred to as "the reed changed to a rock." This comparison may stem from his "bending with the wind" and beginning to sink after Jesus had given him permission to come to Him as he walked on the water. True to his impetuous nature, he got out of the boat and walked successfully until he yielded to fear—took his eyes off the Lord. After refusing to let Jesus wash his feet, he asked that the Master practically give him a bath. He vowed he would die with Christ but, warming himself with the wrong crowd, he denied the Christ three times, just as Jesus had told him he would. He even reverted to his old fisherman's profanity, swearing and cursing at his third denial. I ache with him as Jesus turned and looked directly at him just then. But he did not yield to suicide, as Judas did. His bitter tears manifested his true repentance. He had boldly confessed shortly before the crucifixion that Jesus is the Christ, the Son of God. Endowed with the baptism of the Holy Spirit on the day of Pentecost, he was honored with having his speech recorded as the first gospel sermon. He declared later, "We cannot but speak what we have seen and heard." Finally, he penned two beautiful portions of inspired scripture which speak to us convincingly of "all things that pertain to life and godliness." From a profane fisherman, he grew to such spiritual stature that people brought their sick and laid them on beds and pallets to be healed when Peter's shadow fell on them.

The apostle John is described as intolerant, vindictive, and ambitious. He forbade the casting out of devils by a man who was not following Jesus as he was (Mark 9:38). He and his brother, sometimes called "Sons of Thunder," wanted to call down fire from heaven to burn up people who rejected Jesus (Luke 9:54). They also were ambitious, wanting to be allowed to sit on Jesus' right and left sides when He came in His kingdom. Yet he was referred to often as the apostle whom Jesus loved. We owe to him the book bearing his name, in which so many things Jesus said and did are recorded so that we may have saving faith

(John 20:30,31). Finally, we have him addressing Christians as "my little children," to whom he presents God as the embodiment of love, telling us that we are children of God if we love one another and show our obedient love to God (1, 2, and 3 John). Then he gives us, in Revelation, a peek into heaven and the assurance that God will see that right triumphs over wrong.

We first meet Saul as he consented to the death of the first Christian martyr, Stephen, in Acts 7. He still was "breathing out threatenings and slaughter against the disciples of the Lord" when we next meet him in Acts 9 as he secured permission from the high priest to put Christians to death. The vision in which Jesus asked why Saul was persecuting Him brought the persecutor to his knees asking, "Who are you, Lord?" He did as he was told, was led to Damascus where he fasted and prayed for three days. After Ananias, in obedience to the Lord's direction, had spoken God's Word to him, he arose, was baptized, and was ready to preach the Christ whom he had been persecuting. Much of the rest of the book of Acts tells of his missionary work, and we are deeply indebted to him for a majority of the books of the New Testament, from which we quote so often as we try to understand how the Christian life is to be lived. He described himself as the "chief of sinners," but he became **a living sacrifice**.

> *I thank him who has given me strength for this, Christ Jesus our Lord, because he judged me faithful by appointing me to his service, though I formerly blasphemed and persecuted and insulted him; but I received mercy because I had acted ignorantly in unbelief, and the grace of our Lord overflowed for me with the faith and love that are in Christ Jesus. The saying is sure and worthy of full acceptance, that Christ Jesus came into the world to save sinners. And I am the foremost of sinners, but I received mercy for this reason, that in me, as the foremost, Jesus Christ might display his perfect patience for an example to those who were to believe in him for eternal life (1 Timothy 1:12-16, RSV).*

> *I have been crucified with Christ; it is no longer I who live, but Christ who lives in me; and the life I now live in the flesh I live by faith in the Son of God, who loved me and gave himself for me (Galatians 2:20, RSV).*

In the fourth chapter of John, we have the beautiful story of Jesus' power to reform an alien sinner. He, according to the tradition of the Jews, was supposed to have nothing to do with a Samaritan or even to talk with a woman of that race. Yet He met the Samaritan woman at the well and offered her living water. He didn't hesitate to remind her that

73

she had had five husbands and was living with a man who was not her husband. Rather than being offended, perhaps because of His straightforward, authoritative manner, she recognized Him as a prophet and hastened back to the town to spread the news that a man who might be the Christ of prophecy was waiting at the well. They came and were convinced. At their insistence, He stayed two days longer, and many more believed.

III. In the ugly cocoon of sin in which the Samaritan woman was entwined, Jesus was able to see the beautiful butterfly which could attract others to Himself. Through the inspired word at work in our lives, any sinner, even the "chief of sinners" among us today, can be transformed into a dynamic Christian, through whom many can be led to a triumphant life.

A. We must go to the New Testament to guide us as we are transformed and grow in grace and knowledge. However, from the Old Testament scriptures, to which Christ gave authenticity, we can learn much about God and His lovingkindness toward those who will obey. So many beautiful similies and metaphors depict for us His nature and power:

> *Have you not known? Have you not heard? The Lord is the everlasting God, the Creator of the ends of the earth. He does not faint or grow weary, his understanding is unsearchable. He gives power to the faint, and to him who has no might he increases strength. Even youths shall faint and be weary, and young men shall fall exhausted; but they who wait for the Lord shall renew their strength, they shall mount up with wings like eagles, they shall run and not be weary, they shall walk and not faint (Isaiah 40:28-31, RSV).*

Wait on the Lord! Don't run off and leave Him by following every religious fad which sweeps the nation. Soar with Christ. Remember that He gave the penitent Peter, who had denied Him three times, the glorious opportunity to confess Him again, again, and again. After Jesus' death and resurrection, Peter and the other apostles went fishing! We are not told whether or not they were "waiting on the Lord," but He cooked breakfast for them and invited them to join Him on the beach. Impetuous Peter left the others in the boat and swam to the shore. I am told that Jesus used *agapao,* the Greek word for the kind of love that is unselfish, ready to serve, in asking twice, "Simon, son of John, do you love me more than these?" The word more indicative of tender, undying affection, *phileo,* is used in Christ's third query of Peter and in all three of the apostle's declarations of his love for the Master. Over and over, Peter was given the opportunity to fulfill Jesus' thrice-repeated ad-monition, "Feed my sheep!" (John 21:15-17).

B. Through his great epistles, that same Peter still is feeding the Lord's sheep today. He tells the lowly how to climb: "All of you should be very humble with each other. 'God is against the proud peo-ple, but he gives grace (kindness) to the humble people' (Proverbs 3:34). So be humble under God's powerful hand. Then he will lift you up when the right time comes. Give all your worries to him, because he cares for you" (1 Peter 5:5b-7, ERV).

1. He tells us we may become living stones. His mind may have raced back to his Master's use of two different words meaning stones of contrasting size. He said, "You are Peter," using the word denoting a detached stone that might be thrown easily. But in referring to Peter's confession—"You are the Christ, the Son of the living God"—He promised to build His church on that stone (confession), a mass of rock, a sure foundation (Matthew 16:15-17). However, he used a different word, indicating metaphorically the living stones to be built into a spiritual house:*

> You are coming to the living Stone. Men did not think this Stone was important, but God chose him; he is precious. YOU also are like living stones. God is using you to build a spir-itual house, so that you will be a holy group of priests, offering spiritual sacrifices which God will gladly accept through Jesus Christ. A section in the Scriptures says this: "Listen! I am putting a stone in Jerusalem. He is a chosen, precious cornerstone. The person who believes in him will never be ashamed" (Isaiah 28:16)—1 Peter 2:4-6, SEB.

As living stones, we must know how to behave ourselves in the house of God, which is His church. We surely will not be wreckers, biting and devouring one another, destroying the spiritual house which belongs to God. Instead, as Paul admonished twice in the latter chapters of Romans, we will build each other up, paying especial attention to the weaker members. We will be willing to do whatever is necessary to build them up (Romans 14:19; 15:2).

2. The body of Christ, His church, is built up as each member uses his God-given ability for the good of the whole. We must never forget that our talents vary, but each of us can play an important part in the growth and effectiveness of the church. True, we are indi-vidually responsible to God, to be judged by our own faithfulness.

Vine, op. cit. 302, Vol. 3; 76 Vol. 4.

Yet just as surely as bricks in a building are held together by mortar, we must be held together by love, a corporate body whose purpose is to glorify God through our union with Christ Jesus. Paul makes this very clear:

> Christ appointed apostles, prophets, evangelists, **spiritual** shepherds, and teachers to prepare the holy people for a ministry of service, for building up the body of Christ. How long? Until we are all together. We must be united in our faith and knowledge of the Son of God. We must become **like** a full-grown man, reaching for the greatest potential of Christ.
>
> Then we will not be little children anymore. The waves will not throw us back and forth. We won't be blown away by the winds of **false** teaching which clever men invent to trick people into following error. When we speak the truth with love, we will grow up into Christ in every way. He is the Head. He is the Source. The whole body is joined and held together with each joint that helps it. It grows with love and builds itself up. Each part does its job (Ephesians 4:11-16, SEB).

Conclusion: The power to change hearts and minds, thus changing wicked or misdirected lives, is transmitted from God through His Word. Those thus changed soar like eagles. They are changed from stumbling blocks to stepping stones!

Daily Bible Reading

Sunday
Cleansed, Acceptable Sacrifices
(Psalm 51:1-17)

Monday
Saved to Do Good
(Titus 3:1-11)

Tuesday
Overcoming Trials by Listening and Doing
(James 1:2-26)

Wednesday
God's Powerful Word
(Isaiah 55:6-11)

Thursday
Failing Bodies, Renewed Spirits
(2 Corinthians 4:1-18)

Friday
Chief of Sinners to Living Sacrifice
(1 Timothy 1:12-17; Galatians 2:20)

Saturday
Build That House!
(Ephesians 4:1-32)

Memory Verses

Philippians 4:4-7

Chapter 7

Seek God's Will

Introduction: Actually, when we have learned to resist the world's pattern of living, have our hearts and minds transformed, "Then you will be able to discern the will of God, and to know what is good, acceptable, and perfect" (Romans 12:2c, NEB).

The renewed mind must be able to **discern**—that is, to examine, scrutinize, question—the teaching to which it is being subjected. The purpose is to determine just what is good, acceptable, and perfect in the sight of God. Is it in accord with His will?

You must be aware that within the religious world, even among those who profess belief in Jesus as the Christ, false teachers may arise. You must compare their teachings to God's Word. This is the only way you can reach a saving understanding of God's will. Then you must follow His will, not man's.

I. You can know the will of God. Jesus and His inspired apostles have presented it in a manner that can be understood and obeyed. The seed is available. We must provide the soil! Jesus made this very clear in His explanation of the parable of the sower:

> *The seed is the word of God. Those by the way side are they that hear; then cometh the devil, and taketh away the word out of their hearts, lest they should believe and be saved. They on the rock* ***are they****, which, when they hear, receive the word with joy; and these have no root, which for a while believe, and in time of temptation fall away. And that which fell among thorns are they, which, when they have heard, go forth, and are choked with cares and riches and pleasures of* ***this*** *life, and bring no fruit to perfection. But that on the good ground are they, which in an honest and good heart, having heard the word, keep* ***it****, and bring forth fruit with patience (Luke 8:11-15, KJ).*

A. The expression "God's will" is bandied about rather carelessly in our society. Those, at times, who are trying to console a bereaved person—perhaps one who has lost a stillborn infant or a loved one killed in an automobile accident—feel a natural loss of words. They say, perhaps lamely, "You must accept it as God's will." The destruction of a lush crop of wheat, the demolition of a home, even of a church building, may be dismissed as the will of God. Such statements made to people under emotional stress may destroy faith rather than upbuild it.

It is true that this is God's world. He is all-powerful, knows all about such incidents, and is omnipresent. He could, if He chose, interfere with the laws of nature to prevent such tragedies. We have in the Old Testament numerous records of His doing just that **for a specific purpose**. The ten plagues perpetrated on the Egyptians were for the purpose of showing them that Jehovah is God and to bring glory to His name. Through them, He secured the release of the Israelites. He accompanied them as Moses led them toward the promised land. He worked through Moses to provide food and water for the complaining horde as they traveled through the desert. Again, the manna from heaven and water from the rock were for the purpose of showing the people that He was their God and was with them.

Jesus and the apostles, also the ones on whom the apostles laid their hands, performed many miracles in New Testament times. If you will study the circumstances carefully, you will see that there was a definite purpose in their performance. Jesus was compassionate in opening the eyes of the blind and in feeding the thousands from a small boy's lunch. But His purpose was to prove His divinity as He fulfilled the scriptures. The miracles performed by His followers were to confirm the fact and the authenticity of the Word being taught and recorded.

Through that inspired record, not through our emotions, we can know God's will for us in this day and age. We are given a verified account:

> We told you about the power of our Lord Jesus Christ. We told you about his coming. Those things we told you were not smart stories that people invented. No! We saw the greatness of Jesus with our own eyes. Jesus heard the voice of the Greatest Glory *(**God**).* That was when Jesus received honor and glory from God the Father. The voice said, "This is my Son and I love him. I am very pleased with him." And we heard that voice. It came from heaven while we were with Jesus on the holy mountain.
>
> This makes us more sure about the things the prophets said. And it is good for you to follow closely what the prophets said.

*The things they said are like a light shining in a dark place.
That light shines until the day begins and the morning star rises
in your hearts. Most important, you must understand this: No
prophecy in the Scriptures ever comes from a person's own inter-
pretation. No! No prophecy ever came from what a man wanted
to say. But men were led by the Holy Spirit and spoke things from
God (2 Peter 1:16-21, ERV).*

B. You must **seek** the truth. You might find a lost article
accidentally, but you certainly are more likely to find it if you look for it.
You even move any obstacles to the search. In the same way, you
should remove prejudice from your mind and really hear what the scriptures are saying to you. I have known, personally, several people who
were diligent in their study of the Bible and were led from denominational error to the truth. One man was so overjoyed that he exclaimed
to his wife, "I have found some people who teach the Bible just as it is!"
He loaded his young wife and their small children into the farm wagon,
forded a river, and took them to hear the truth he had discovered.
That night, they became children of God, and He added them to the
church Jesus built, as He promised. Yes, that was in the horse-and-
buggy days, and those two have gone to their reward, but it is happen-
ing in our space age, too. My husband and I have been worshiping with
a young man who found the Lord's church in precisely the same way.
He and his girlfriend became dissatisfied with the church they were attending when they saw conflicts between its teaching and the New Testament they were reading together. They visited churches until they
found one, when they had almost given up, that taught the truth.
No, they didn't marry, but he enrolled in a Christian college and found a
wife who is his enthusiastic helper in the Lord.

1. In the sermon on the mount, Jesus taught this
principle of being a seeker. He said, "So, I tell you, continue asking and
it will be given to you. Keep on searching and you will find. Be knocking, and the door will open for you. You will receive if you will always
ask. You will find, if you continue looking. And the door will open
for you, if you continue knocking" (Matthew 7:7,8, SEB).

Recently, I heard a preacher say that it is impossible to teach a person
to the extent of obedience if he is not seeking the truth. We must seek
truth continually. Are you seeking?

2. But someone may ask, as Pilate did when the accused Savior stood before him, "What is truth?" Jesus had explained
that His purpose for coming into the world was to bear witness to the
truth. Surely Pilate recognized the ring of truth in Jesus' majestic bearing
and speech. He confessed to the mob outside that he found no fault in

Jesus. He offered to release the accused, but the violent throng chose a robber instead. We want to condemn those people for their blindness to the truth, but we can be just as guilty if we fail to hear what Jesus is saying to us through the New Testament.

Jesus had said to Thomas, "I am the way, and the truth, and the life; no one comes to the Father, but by me" (John 14:6, RSV). To know the truth is to know Jesus. This is not accomplished by some flash of revelation, but by reading His biographers—Matthew, Mark, Luke, and John.

In John 1:1,14, Jesus is identified as the Word which was made flesh and dwelt among us. Of course, that was Jesus, God's means of communicating with us. However, it is not inconsistent with that teaching when Jesus, in His beautiful prayer just before His crucifixion, identifies the truth further: "Sanctify them through thy truth: thy word is truth" (John 17:17, KJ). By that Word, the truth, we can be made holy, set apart for the Master's use!

C. As we read God's Word, we see numbers of things He wants. We will discuss only a few of them here, but you can refresh your mind frequently as you discover more and more of His will. Jesus told a parable of a man who had 100 sheep, and one of them got lost. He left the 99 and went to look for the poor little stray. When he found it, he rejoiced over the one that had been found more than the others that were not lost. Jesus was emphasizing God's concern for even a little child: "So it is not the will of my Father who is in heaven that one of these little ones should perish" (Matthew 18:14, RSV).

Peter said it this way: "God doesn't want any person to be lost. God wants every person to change his heart and stop sinning" (2 Peter 3:9b, ERV).

D. As we fill our hearts and minds with God's Word, worldly thoughts and temptations will be crowded out. As we learn to enjoy discovering His will in the Word, we will find pleasure in obedience. David expressed many times his joy in pleasing God: "I delight to do thy will, O my God: yea, thy law is within my heart" (Psalm 40:8, KJ). And again he said, "With my whole heart have I sought thee: O let me not wander from thy commandments. Thy word have I hid in mine heart, that I might not sin against thee" (Psalm 119:10,11, KJ). Throughout the Bible, we learn that God wanted trust and obedience.

II. As we grow spiritually, we will be able to discern—that is, to examine—various teachings to determine if they are good, acceptable, and perfect. Knowledge both of the facts being considered and of God's Word is necessary to a Christian's judgment of a situation. Paul prayed that the Philippian Christians might make the right choices:

I want your love to overflow more and more with fuller knowl-
edge and all insight. Then you will be able to test what is best, so
you will be pure and without guilt when Christ comes. You will be
filled with what righteousness produces through Jesus Christ for
the glory and praise of God (Philippians 1:9-11, SEB).

We have noted a tendency in this age toward an emotional love toward God and others which might blind us to truth. Certainly, we are to love God and one another, to be kindly affectioned toward each other. But we must possess the knowledge to recognize and approve the highest and the best. Application of these things to our lives will free us from guilt and fill us with true goodness available to us in Jesus Christ.

In writing to Timothy, Paul affirms that a knowledge of the inspired scriptures can make us wise, help us to be saved and furnished to every good work:

You have known the Holy Scriptures since you were a child.
Those Scriptures are able to make you wise. And that wisdom
leads to salvation through faith in Christ Jesus. All Scripture
is given by God. And all Scripture is useful for teaching and
for showing people the things that are wrong in their lives. It is
useful for correcting faults, and teaching how to live right. Using
the Scriptures, the person who serves God will be ready and will
have everything he needs to do every good work (2 Timothy
3:15-17, ERV).

Other translations say the scriptures can equip the man of God so that he may be perfect, complete, right, and efficient. One describes the scriptures as the comprehensive equipment of the man of God.

Jesus is the example of the perfect life. We have noted that He came to do God's will, that in His teaching He was dependent on God. He said to Philip, "Do you not believe that I am in the Father and the Father in me? The words that I say to you I do not speak on my own authority; but the Father who dwells in me does his works. Believe me that I am in the Father and the Father in me; or else believe me for the sake of the works themselves" (John 14:10,11, RSV).

We are told that Jesus, our great High Priest, was tempted in every way that we are, yet He never sinned (Hebrews 4:15). His trust always was in God and became the perfect example and sacrifice for our sins:

*He (**Christ**) did no sin, and no lies were found in his mouth*
(Isaiah 53:9).

People said bad things to Christ, but he did not say bad things to
them. Christ suffered, but he did not threaten (speak against) the

people. No! Christ let God take care of him. God is the One who judges rightly. Christ carried our sins in his body on the cross. He did this so that we would stop living for sin and live for what is right (1 Peter 2:22-24b, ERV).

III. We must be just as careful to avoid false religious teaching as we are to follow our perfect example, Jesus Christ. Again, we go to His sermon on the mount for a warning: "Beware of false prophets, which come to you in sheep's clothing, but inwardly they are ravening wolves. Ye shall know them by their fruits. Do men gather grapes of thorns, or figs of thistles?" (Matthew 7:15,16, KJ). The air waves are full of religious teaching, especially on Sunday. Since they, at times, present conflicting teaching, how are we to know what is right? We must not be gullible, but be careful to compare their product to the spiritual fruit produced by a life in accord with Christ's teaching. Solomon described a person who would believe just anything as simple:

The simple believes everything, but the prudent looks where he is going. A wise man is cautious and turns away from evil, but a fool throws off restraint and is careless" (Proverbs 14:15,16, RSV).

A. You may say, "But those people are so sincere. Their services make me feel good. I enjoy the choir and the organ accompaniment." When the Israelites were occupying the promised land, they made a grave mistake of judging by appearances and failing to ask God's guidance. The residents of Gibeon had heard that God had delivered Jericho and Ai into the hands of the Israelites, also that He had commanded them to destroy all the inhabitants of the land. They devised a cunning plan to trick the armies led by Joshua. Donning worn-out clothing, they loaded stale provisions and cracked wineskins on their asses and presented themselves as having come from afar. The Israelites took them at their word without asking directions from God. After making a covenant with them, to which Israel's leaders swore, they learned that they were their neighbors. The people murmured, but Joshua and the leaders would not go back on their oath. The Gibeonites became woodcutters and slaves. The Israelites finally were led into idolatry and disobedience by the aliens living among them and were eventually led into captivity (Joshua 9:3-26).

B. On several occasions, Paul warned against false teachers. In his farewell to the elders from Ephesus, he cautioned, "Take heed to yourselves and to all the flock, in which the Holy Spirit has made you guardians, to feed the church of the Lord which he obtained with his own blood. I know that after my departure fierce wolves will come in among you, not sparing the flock; and from among your own selves will arise men speaking perverse things, to draw away the disciples after them" (Acts 20:28-30, RSV). He wrote that church later:

Don't let anyone fool you with empty words. This is why God's punishment is coming against people who won't obey. So, don't take part in these things with them.

In the past you were in darkness, but now, you are in light, in the Lord Jesus. Live like children of light, because the light produces all kinds of goodness, righteousness, and truth. Test *everything* to see if it would please the Lord (Ephesians 5:6-10, SEB).

IV. We are accustomed to standards whereby we know when we are receiving full measure in things we purchase. You may even gather a handful of material and give it a hard squeeze to see if it is wrinkle-resistant. You smear a small amount of foundation lotion on your wrist to see if it is the right shade. Use the same method in testing religious teaching. Compare it with God's Word. Some will not do so, for they do not want to risk being upset. They may even recognize their error but refuse to change from a false concept of loyalty to their parents. They may choose to follow their own consciences or feelings rather than the truth they see in the scriptures. Jesus said that some would stop their ears so that they could not hear and close their eyes so that they could not see. He said they would be lost. He was quoting Isaiah 6:9,10, as recorded in Matthew 13:14,15.

A. If God had made us robots whom He subjected to His will by the press of a button, it would not be necessary for us to discern good and evil. Since we are accountable human beings, we must learn to use the judgment He has given us so that we may know His will and obey it. We must keep what is in accordance with that will and discard all that is not:

Prove all things; hold fast that which is good (1 Thessalonians 5:21, KJ).

My dear **friends**, many false prophets are now in the world. So don't believe every spirit. Test the spirits to see whether they are from God. This is how you can recognize God's Spirit: One Spirit says, "I believe that Jesus is the Christ. Jesus came to earth and became a human being." That spirit is from God. Another spirit refuses to say this about Jesus. That spirit is not from God. This is the spirit of the enemy of Christ. You have heard he was coming and now he is already in the world!

85

My little children, you belong to God. You have conquered the **false prophets**, *because the One that is in you is greater than the one who is in the people of the world. Those false prophets belong to the world. The world listens to what they say. We are from God. The people who know God listen to us, but the people who are not from God don't listen to us. That is how we can recognize the Spirit who is true and the spirit who is false (1 John 4:1-6, SEB).*

We note that those who recognize Jesus Christ as God's Son who came to earth to fulfill God's eternal purpose are of God. Those who refuse to make this confession are of the world, not of God. Notice, also, that those who are of God listen to His spokesmen. Again, we must go to a familiar scripture to ascertain the true meaning of claiming Jesus as Lord:

Not every person who says that I am his Lord will enter the kingdom of heaven. The only people who will enter the kingdom of heaven are those people who do the things that my Father in heaven wants. On the last day, many people will say to me, "You are our Lord! We spoke for you. And for you we forced out demons and did many miracles." Then I will tell those people clearly, "Go away from me, you people that do wrong. I never knew you" (Matthew 7:21-23, ERV).

B. As we have indicated, we must clear the channels of our minds so that God's message will not be hindered in reaching our understanding. Our own attitudes may defeat the Lord's purpose in our lives. Paul recognized that Timothy, in preaching the Word, would need urgency in convincing and, if necessary, correcting those whom he taught. He would need to be patient because some people might not be in the most receptive mood: "The time will come when people will not listen to the true teaching. But people will find more and more teachers that please them. People will find teachers that say the things those people want to hear. People will stop listening to the truth. They will begin to follow the teaching in false stories" (2 Timothy 4:3,4, ERV).

C. Luke tells us in Acts 17:10-12 of some people who were good listeners; in fact, they were searchers for the truth. Not willing to accept the word even of Paul and Silas without confirmation, they searched the scriptures daily to see if what they had heard so eagerly really were true. As a result, many of them believed and became Christians. They were called more noble than those in Thessalonica because of their "readiness of mind" and their study of the scriptures.

May we who have God's revealed will so readily available be as noble and open-minded as were the Bereans! Don't hesitate to compare what you hear from a pulpit or on radio or television with the written Word.

D. We can assume that most people who would teach us false doctrine are sincere. They may simply have been misled by a false teacher. There may, however, be some, like the Jewish leaders, who know and even believe the truth but, because of their position in the world, continue in error. It hurts when we must reject the teaching of a loved one or a respected teacher or preacher, but we must have the courage to do so when we learn that God's Word does not agree with what we have been taught. You will find spiritual companionship greater than earthly ties. Jesus promised that those who have left fathers or mothers, children, brothers, sisters, or lands for His sake will have more now and, in the world to come, eternal life (Mark 10:29,30).

The Jews learned the hard way the penalty of disobeying God's instructions. We can avoid that sentence if we are diligent in learning God's will and accepting it in spite of what any person may say to the contrary. Paul admonished:

> What then? If some did not believe, their unbelief will not nullify the faithfulness of God, will it? May it never be! Rather, let God be found true, though every man be found a liar, as it is written, "THAT THOU MIGHTEST BE JUSTIFIED IN THY WORDS, AND MIGHTEST PREVAIL WHEN THOU ART JUDGED" (Psalm 51:4) — Romans 3:3,4, NASV.

Conclusion: You **can** know and follow God's will. You will grow spiritually as you feed on His Word. Beware of remaining immature! You must engage in spiritual exercise to develop the maturity that will allow you to understand the "solid food" of God's Word. Grow up!

> About this we have much to say which is hard to explain, since you have become dull of hearing. For though by this time you ought to be teachers, you need some one to teach you again the first principles of God's word. You need milk, not solid food; for every one who lives on milk is unskilled in the word of righteousness, for he is a child. But solid food is for the mature, for those who have their faculties trained by practice to distinguish good from evil (Hebrews 5:11-14, RSV).

Daily Bible Reading

Sunday
Provide Good Soil!
(Luke 8:4-15)

Monday
Listen to An Eyewitness!
(2 Peter 1:12-21)

Tuesday
Seek and You Will Find!
(Matthew 7:7,8; John 17:17)

Wednesday
Develop Insight!
(Philippians 1:9-11)

Thursday
Be Thoroughly Equipped!
(2 Timothy 3:15-17)

Friday
Don't Let Anyone Fool You!
(Ephesians 5:6-10)

Saturday
Grow Up!
(Hebrews 5:7-14)

Memory Verses

Matthew 7:7,8

John 17:17

Chapter 8

Look in God's Mirror

Introduction: Have you been through a house of mirrors? If so, you will remember how some of them distorted you; you were extremely tall or short or out of proportion. It all depended on the particular mirror in which you were looking. You may actually have hurried to a true mirror to confirm your usual, pleasing image.

In the same way, the mirrors of the world can distort the Christian you. You may receive praise to the extent that you "think of yourself more highly than you ought to think." You may be belittled until you feel you have no worth at all.

God's Word is the true mirror. We get a true evaluation of self as a Christian through its reflection. As a child of God, you have great worth. Things often are valued by the price paid for them. **You** were purchased with the precious blood of Christ!

We still must wrestle, though, with our human ego reflected by the world's mirror. Just as Satan tempted Eve by telling her she would be wise like God after eating the forbidden fruit, he may, through others, give us an inflated image of ourselves. We may become proud, haughty, and conceited.

Jesus can help us maintain our spiritual equilibrium as we realize we are part of His body, using the gifts God has given us for the well-being of the whole. As we humble ourselves, God will exalt us!

I. Don't cherish exaggerated ideas of yourself or your importance. In much of his letter to the Romans, it seems that Paul was trying to persuade them to see themselves as Christians, freed from the old law, no longer privileged Jews or alien Gentiles. We are heirs of the same privilege, not because of anything we have done, but because of God's grace extended to us through Jesus Christ. We are in constant need of Paul's admonition, too: "Through God's gracious love which has been given to me, I am telling each of you, don't think you are bet-

ter than you really are. Instead, be modest in the way you think"
(Romans 12:3, SEB).

A. Human nature has not changed; it is natural for us to
want to be classed with those in high position. Apparently, kings of old
seated their guests according to their rank. It was extremely embar-
rassing for one who had taken his position near the head of the table to
be asked to move down to make way for a nobler person. Solomon
warned:

> Do not put yourself forward in the king's presence or stand in
> the place of the great; for it is better to be told, "Come up here,"
> than to be put lower in the presence of the prince (Proverbs
> 25:6,7, RSV).

B. Jesus mirrored human behavior and taught many practical lessons in His parables. His stories were never for mere entertain-
ment. They always had a point just as applicable to us today as it was to
certain people who were confident of their own goodness and looked
down on others:

> Two men went up into the temple to pray; the one a Pharisee,
> and the other a publican. The Pharisee stood and prayed thus
> with himself, God, I thank thee, that I am not as other men are,
> extortioners, unjust, adulterers, or even as this publican. I fast
> twice in the week, I give tithes of all that I possess. And the
> publican, standing afar off, would not lift up so much as his eyes
> unto heaven, but smote upon his breast, saying, God be merciful
> to me a sinner. I tell you, this man went down to his house justi-
> fied rather than the other: for every one that exalteth himself shall
> be abased; and he that humbleth himself shall be exalted (Luke
> 18:10-14, KJ).

By our actions, others can see how good, or bad, we are. We certainly have no need to inform God! It is our **good works**, prompted by
love and reverence for God and His will, that convey our light to the
world. Jesus said, "You are the light of the world. A city set on a hill
cannot be hid. Nor do men light a lamp and put it under a bushel, but
on a stand, and it gives light to all in the house. Let your light so shine
before men, that they may see your good works and give glory to your
Father who is in heaven" (Matthew 5:14-16, RSV). False modesty
should not prompt us to hide our good deeds; neither are we to shout
them from the housetop. Remember the children's song: "This little
light of mine; I'm gonna let it shine! Put it under a bushel? No! I'm gonna
let it shine!"

C. Our aim in living a sacrificial life is to be like Jesus. He described Himself as meek and lowly in heart, or gentle and humble-hearted (Matthew 11:29b). During the Last Supper, He gave His apostles a dynamic illustration of His own humility. He knew that His crucifixion was near. He knew, also, that those near and dear to Him needed the lesson. He removed His outer garments, girded Himself with a towel, and washed their feet. He had explained that they would not understand just then what He was doing, but later they would understand. After reclothing Himself, He sat down with them and said, "Do you know what I have just done to you? You call me 'Teacher' and 'Lord.' You are right, because I am the Teacher and the Lord. Since I, the Lord and Teacher, washed your feet, you ought to wash one another's feet. I have given you an example. You should do things *for others* as I have done for you" (John 13:12c-15, SEB).

No task performed for others because of our love for Jesus should be beneath our dignity. Like our Teacher and Master, we should be willing to serve each other in menial ways.

II. Jesus' strength, even His humility, came from His close relationship with His Father. He knew where He came from and where He was going: "The Father had given Jesus power over everything. Jesus knew this. Jesus also knew that He had come from God. And He knew that He was going back to God" (John 13:3, ERV). As members of the Lord's body, the church, we share a common destiny. To reach that goal of joining Jesus in heaven, we must function as a vital part of that body, just as the members of our physical body each has its own task to perform for the good of the whole. There should be no rivalry between us as we find our mission according to the talent, or nature, given us by the Lord. Paul makes this very clear:

> Each one of us has one body and that body has many parts. These parts don't all do the same thing. In the same way, we are many people, but in Christ we are all one body. We are the parts of that body. And each part of that body belongs to all the other parts. We all have different gifts. Each gift came because of the grace (**kindness**) that God gave us. If a person has the gift of prophecy, then that person should use that gift with the faith he has. If a person has the gift of serving, then that person should serve. If a person has the gift of teaching, then that person should teach. If a person has the gift of comforting other people, then that person should comfort. If a person has the gift of giving to help other people, then that person should give freely. If a person has the gift of being a leader, then that person should work hard when he leads. If a person has the gift of showing kindness to

other people, then that person should do that with joy (Romans 12:4-8, ERV).

It is not our purpose here to study in detail each of these ministries. We do want to emphasize that an effort should be made by our leaders to know where we can best serve the whole. We also should take a candid look at ourselves and devote ourselves wholeheartedly to serving in our own realm. Our concern should never be who gets the glory—that belongs to God through Jesus Christ!

Flavil Yeakley Jr. predicts that in time we will see churches employing skilled workers whose task is to direct the members in finding and using their ministries. In fact, he says some already are gaining strength and outreach through such an effort. This, he says, would eliminate the "shotgun" appeals from the pulpit, urging every member to become involved in a particular ministry. If the appeal is for home Bible teachers, some conscientious souls will surely feel guilty in not responding to a challenge for which they are not suited. Rather, the director of ministries would go to those who have the talent and have developed the ability to perform that service, show them the need, and encourage them as they work.

Some women are not able to withstand the depressing or upsetting task of ministering to the disoriented or ailing in nursing homes. They should leave that work to those who find joy in bringing just a bit of sunshine into a troubled life. I am thinking of a lovely sister in Christ, the wife of an elder, whose sympathetic nature was so touched that she was unable to share the good lunch tray provided by the nursing home; while another sister was able to feed a patient whose every swallow was an effort, then enjoy eating food prepared by others. The elder's wife, however, was a beautiful example of a loving, caring helper suited to him. She worked effectively as a teacher in the primary department of the Bible school, and was able to train other teachers while acting as that department's supervisor.

Had you ever thought of the ability to give as a talent? There are those who find fulfillment in a nine-to-five job with benefits including good vacations. They have the time and may develop the talent to be skilled teachers or excellent comforters. Others have the ability to make money; they can be effective ministers, giving freely! Still others can be cheerful in their kindness to those in need, physically or spiritually. The work of the body is accomplished as each uses his talent faithfully and freely with hard work, diligence, zeal, and cheerfulness.

III. Paul could not have pictured real Christian behavior without including brotherly love. This love must be genuine. We women may be happy to wear costume jewelry, which never is intended to do other

92

than accent our dress. We would never think of trying to pass it off as a real diamond or ruby. However, imitation love is hypocrisy. Remember how scathingly Jesus reprimanded the Pharisees as hypocrites (Matthew 23) and Paul characterized the ultimate sacrifice without love as **nothing** (1 Corinthians 13). Our love for each other must be as genuine and unselfish as that which Jesus manifested toward us while we were yet sinners. He gave us a new command:

> I love you, just as the Father loves me. Stay in my love. I have obeyed my Father's commands and I stay in his love. If you obey my commands, you will stay in my love.
>
> I have said these things to you, so that my joy may be in you and your joy may be complete. This is my command: Love one another, as I have loved you. Suppose someone gives up his life for his friends. No one has a greater love than this. You are my friends, if you do what I tell you to do . . . Love one another! I am ordering you to do this (John 15:9-14,17, SEB).

A. Jesus described brotherly love as the distinguishing characteristic of the Christian. This love, manifested in His body, lets the world know that we are His disciples: "By this all men will know that you are my disciples, if you have love for one another" (John 13:35, RSV).

Brotherly kindness and love top the list of the Christian graces itemized by Peter (2 Peter 1:5-7). He urged that we make every effort to add these qualities to our faith. If they abound in our lives, we will be neither complacent or ineffective as Christians. If we lack them, we are described as blind, shortsighted, having forgotten the wonderful blessing of being cleansed from sin.

1. This must be a genuine love: "Let love be without dissimulation" (Romans 12:9a, KJ). The adjective used here is closely related to the noun in the Greek which originated as the acting of a stage player, hence pretense. Other translations say "Let love be genuine" (RSV), "Love in all sincerity" (NEV), and "Your love must be real" (ERV). Actually, the bond of love between Christians is stronger than that between brothers and sisters in the flesh. It will last through eternity.

2. This brotherly love is not to be a cold ritual, a limp handshake, and a muttered "How'r ya?" It includes warmth, affection, genuine concern. It is interesting that Peter links obedience to the truth **unto** a sincere love of the brethren: "Seeing ye have purified your souls in obeying the truth through the Spirit unto unfeigned love of the brethren, see that ye love one another with a pure heart fervently" (1 Peter 1:22, KJ). The Revised Standard says, "Having purified your souls by your obedience to the truth for a sincere love of the brethren, love one another earnestly from the heart" (op. cit.). In the same verse, the New English makes a distinct connection between purification of the souls and brotherly love: "Now that by obedience to the truth you have purified your souls until you feel sincere affection towards your brother Christians, love one another wholeheartedly with all your strength." Our Christian love is to be wholehearted, warm, with pure affection.

   3. We are not to be stingy in our love for one another. It should overflow. This kind of love will not be characterized as a clique, a tight little group alike in social standing, shutting out those who differ. Surely, it has room for close friends among fellow Christians, but it is so abundant that it engulfs the new Christian, the weak, the unlovely. More than one of Paul's epistles to the churches opens with his prayer for this kind of love: "May the Lord make your love grow and overflow to one another and everyone else, just as our love does toward you" (1 Thessalonians 3:12, SEB).

   B. Unselfish Christian love makes us happy to see a brother or sister given honor above ourself. The King James says, "In honour preferring one another" (Romans 12:9c). At times, this has been interpreted as giving our business to our brethren. Although this text may not teach just that, we should, out of love for each other, be willing to help in every way. And we can rest assured that a dollar spent with one of our fellow Christians will help him to be liberal in his giving to the Lord.

   "Outdo one another in showing honor" is the wording in the Revised Standard Version. This kind of rivalry surely is pleasing to the Lord. The New English says, "Give pride of place to one another in esteem." The Easy-to-Read Version says, "You should want to give your brothers and sisters more honor than you want for yourself."

   IV. As Christians, we are to live in harmony. There is no room for snobbery or conceit; these do not characterize real Christian behavior. Paul encouraged, "Live in harmony with one another; do not be haughty, but associate with the lowly; never be conceited" (Romans 12:16, RSV).

   A. Our confidence is in Christ, and we can be humbly grateful to be called "children of God." But we must be ever on the alert to avoid being puffed up with worldly pride. Remembering that our talents and abilities are given to us, we will be thankful rather than proud. The wise man warned against fleshly pride: "Pride goes before destruction, and a haughty spirit before a fall" (Proverbs 16:18, RSV).

   B. Just as a discord in music grates on the ear, lack of harmony among Christians will cause outsiders, even weak brothers and sisters, to turn away in disgust. Paul warned, "But if you bite and devour one another take heed that you are not consumed by one another" (Galatians 5:15, RSV). He had admonished the Roman Christians, "Live together in peace" (Romans 12:16b, ERV).

Harmony, even in singing gospel songs, can attract others. I know a strong Christian young man who said a friend invited him first to attend services to enjoy the beautiful singing. He came and saw the beauty of harmonious, happy Christian lives. He studied the scriptures, became a Christian, found a wife who shared his trust in the Lord, and established a Christian home.

C. Being a Christian is an exalted privilege, a high calling. In our business, social and family life, we should never forget who we are. We must behave in a manner that will attract others to the Lord. Certainly, we will want to do nothing that will drive others away, give them a reason to say, "If that is a Christian, I want none of it!"

Paul pleads with us to behave as Christians should:

> I therefore, a prisoner for the Lord, beg you to lead a life worthy of the calling to which you have been called, with all lowliness and meekness, with patience, forbearing one another in love, eager to maintain the unity of the Spirit, in the bond of peace (Ephesians 4:1-3, RSV).

D. There is no such thing as an unimportant child of God. Each was bought with the same precious blood. Even those who have not become followers of Christ possess an immortal soul said to be more valuable than the whole world. In Romans 12:16, the King James Version tells us to "condescend to men of low estate." I like the Phillip Version which says, "Take a real interest in ordinary people." Perhaps the latter conveys more clearly the true meaning of the scripture, for to condescend infers that we are exalted. This is true only if we have humbled ourselves and let God do the exalting!

Snobbery never mixes well with faith. The Book of James has been called one of practical Christianity. He gets right to the point in this matter:

> My brethren, show no partiality as you hold the faith of our Lord Jesus Christ, the Lord of glory. For if a man with gold rings and in fine clothing comes into your assembly, and a poor man in shabby clothing also comes in, and you pay attention to the one who wears the fine clothing and say, "Have a seat here, please," while you say to the poor man, "Stand there," or, "Sit at my feet," have you not made distinctions among yourselves, and become judges with evil thoughts? Listen, my beloved brethren. Has not God chosen those who are poor in the world to be rich in

faith and heirs of the kingdom which he has promised to those who love him? (James 2:1-5, RSV).

E. Paul ends his appeal for humility with a terse "Don't be conceited" (Romans 12:16c, ERV). The King James says, "Be not wise in your own conceits." We are told that the wisdom of man is foolishness with God. Therefore, if we glory in our earthly wisdom, we are deceiving ourselves. There is really no one more apt to be ridiculed than the person who thinks he is "somebody" when he really is nothing. This thought was made very clear long ago: "Do you see a man who is wise in his own eyes? There is more hope for a fool than for him" (Proverbs 26:12, RSV). One who trusts in her own wisdom sees no reason to seek God. She will not learn the truth that will make her really wise unto salvation.

Conclusion: Someone said that with God, the way up is down. We must learn our true value through looking in God's mirror. Like Jesus, we must be meek and lowly. We will find our true value in being a part of Christ's body, performing our ministry with the gifts He has given us, strengthening the whole. Our sincere love for one another will lead us to honor others above self. We will not be proud or conceited, but will show real interest in all our brothers and sisters in Christ. We will heed Peter's admonition:

> *Everyone should be humble with one another. Wear humility like a covering, because the scripture says: "God is against those who are proud, but he gives help to humble people" (Proverbs 3:34). So, make yourselves humble under God's powerful hand. Then, at the right time, he will lift you up. Throw all your worries onto God, because he cares for you (1 Peter 5:5b-7, SEB).*

Daily Bible Reading

Sunday
An Appropriate Parable
(Luke 18:10-14)

Monday
Real Christian Living
(Romans 12)

Tuesday
An Example to Follow
(John 13:1-15)

Wednesday
Find Your Ministry
(Romans 12:4-8)

Thursday
Jesus, the True Vine
(John 15:1-17)

Friday
Unto Love of the Brethren
(1 Peter 1:22, 1 Thessalonians 3:12)

Saturday
Show No Partiality
(James 2:1-13)

Memory Verses

1 Peter 5:5-10

Chapter 9

Zealous and Glowing

Introduction: A sacrificial life is one filled with industry, enthusiasm, and service. Remembering God's gracious love which lifted us from sin to salvation through the sacrifice of His son, Jesus Christ, we consider ourselves, like Paul, crucified with Christ. Yet we live because Christ lives in us. As we grasp the magnanimity of our new life, we are prompted, as David said, to cry:

> Righteous art thou, O Lord, and right are thy judgments. Thou hast appointed thy testimonies in righteousness and in all faithfulness. My zeal consumes me, because my foes forget thy words. Thy promise is well tried, and thy servant loves it. I am small and despised, yet I do not forget thy precepts. Thy righteousness is righteous for ever, and thy law is true. Trouble and anguish have come upon me, but thy commandments are my delight. Thy testimonies are righteous for ever; give me understanding that I may live (Psalm 119:137-144, RSV).

Without Christ, I am small and despised. Yet, as I delight in the law of the Lord, in keeping His commandments, I am rewarded with this magnanimity—this loftiness of spirit enabling me to bear trouble calmly, to disdain meanness and revenge, and to sacrifice my life in zeal for good works, serving the Lord.

    I. One characteristic of real Christian behavior is sustained enthusiasm. We are cautioned not to grow weary in well-doing. Paul says, "Never flag in zeal" (Romans 12:11a, RSV). In other words, don't become lazy or fail to pace yourself so that you will not fall victim to "burnout."

        A. We must avoid being slothful Christians. Sadly, we have seen new converts ready to "take the world for Christ" lapse into indifference or actually fall away. What happened? Were they discouraged at the sight of older Christians still so immature that they could not share the good works proposed by the novice? Were they given tasks requiring skills beyond their growth? Were they lulled into indifference by a congregation drifting along without positive spiritual goals? Did the leaders fail to give them **anything** to do? Did they fall asleep spiritually? Among Solomon's proverbs is the warning, "Slothfulness casts into a deep sleep, and an idle person will suffer hunger" (Proverbs 19:15, RSV).

    1. Leaders often are discouraged and programs fail because they are met with excuses rather than enthusiasms. It isn't hard at all to find an excuse if one really is indifferent, really does not want to work. We can fill our life with previous plans which may include "make work" activities. We may have a convenient headache. We may become too involved in worldly activities, some of which may be good in themselves if they do not absorb so much of our energy and time we have none left for the Lord's work. Surely we will not resort to some bugaboo of our own imagination such as we read of in Proverbs 22:13, RSV: "The sluggard says, 'There is a lion outside! I shall be slain in the streets!' "

    2. Both physical and spiritual poverty may overtake the indolent. Effort is required as we are providing the everyday needs of our families for food and clothing. When Jesus warned that we should not make those things of first importance in our lives—worry about them—He did not mean that we were to be lazy.

We do not grow spiritually just by wishing we knew as much about the Bible as some older Christian does. Remember, Peter said "give all diligence" to add the Christian graces, enumerated in 2 Peter 1, to our lives. A lazy farmer's field soon is overgrown with weeds. An indifferent Christian's mind may be filled with useless trivia, worldly goals. A rock fence may tumble down because of its owner's indolence. A neighbor's livestock may wander in and destroy even the crop left by the weeds. We are told to be watchful, to resist, even to flee from temptation. We can become careless, lower our guard, and our spiritual zeal may be quenched by worldly cares and temptations. Again, we go to Proverbs for a warning:

> I passed by the field of a sluggard, by the vineyard of a man without sense; and lo, it was all overgrown with thorns; the ground was covered with nettles, and its stone wall was broken down. Then I saw and considered it; I looked and received instruction. A little sleep, a little slumber, a little folding of the hands to rest, and poverty will come upon you like a robber, and want like an armed man (Proverbs 24:30-34, RSV).

There are times when we should confront temptation. Both Peter and James tell us to resist the devil and he will flee from us (1 Peter 5:9; James 4:7). Jesus warned the apostles to watch lest they enter into temptation (Matthew 26:41). Paul warned men of God to run from or flee the tantalizing pull of the love of money (1 Timothy 6:11, KJ). If we are slothful or indifferent, we may just sit and let temptation overcome us!

B. We must overcome inertia by being zealous in our Christian lives. Peter assured us that the Lord wants all of us to come to repentance, thus avoiding the punishment which awaits the unrighteous. But he also cautioned that we dare not put off matters pertaining to our salvation because the day of the Lord will come as a thief in the night, without warning. He asks, in view of the facts, "What sort of persons ought you to be in lives of holiness and godliness?" Then he concludes, "Therefore, beloved, since you wait for these, be zealous to be found by him without spot or blemish, and at peace" (2 Peter 3:11b,14, RSV).

1. You may be a younger woman, thinking that there is plenty of time for you to become concerned about spiritual growth and activity. You should have more time than I have left, but we have no assurance of that. I am planning right now to finish this chapter, then take a walk, but I am not sure that this will be accomplished. We are advised to live one day at a time, and that is good. But actually, we live only one heartbeat at a time! So I do plan to be diligent in my study of God's Word and my effort to help you to love it and apply it to your life. I pray that, if the Lord wills, you may live to be a better Bible student than I and that your life will encourage still younger women to be enthusiastic Christians. May we both heed Solomon's admonition to use well the time we have: "Whatever thy hand findeth to do, do it with thy might; for there is no work, nor device, nor knowledge, nor wisdom, in the grave, whither thou goest" (Ecclesiastes 9:10, KJ).

2. While undergoing hardships which few, if any, of us will have to face, Paul set an example of untiring zeal. He worked hard for the cause to which he was dedicated, for which he was even willing to give his life. Often his heart was heavy as he prayed earnestly for the Israelites, his own countrymen. He worked just as diligently as the special messenger to the Gentiles. From his own writing, we can see an example which we can follow with confidence:

Brothers, you know that our stay among you was a success. Before we arrived there, as you know, we had suffered and had been insulted in the city of Philippi. But with our God's help, we dared to tell you God's Good News, even when some people strongly opposed us. Our plea does not come from false, impure, or tricky motives. No, we talk like men who have been tested by God. He trusted us with the Good News. We don't talk like men who are trying to please men. No, God tests our hearts. In the past, you know we never used flattery. We didn't try to look good, only to get your money. God knows this is true! We were not looking for glory from men — not from you or anyone else.

As Christ's apostles, we could have been hard on you, but we were gentle among you, like a mother taking care of her children. We loved you very much. It was a pleasure to share with you not only God's Good News, but also our lives. You had become precious to us. Brothers, do you remember our hard work? We were exhausted. We worked night and day; we didn't want to be a burden to you while we preached God's Good News to you.

We were pure, righteous, and without guilt among you believers. You know it and God knows it! You know that we treated each one of you as a father treats his own children. We encouraged you, comforted you, and told you to live your lives worthy of God who called you into His kingdom and glory (1 Thessalonians 2:1-12, SEB).

3. In encouraging those to whom he preached, Paul used as examples congregations and individual Christians. He was a great motivator, using psychology at its best. He knew that those to whom he wrote would want to live up to his confidence in them: "Therefore openly before the churches show them the proof of your love and of our reason for boasting about you. For it is superfluous for me to write to you about this ministry to the saints; for I know your readiness, of which I boast about you to the Macedonians, namely, that Achaia has been prepared since last year, and your zeal has stirred up most of them" (2 Corinthians 8:24—9:2, NASV).

He sent greetings to the Christians at Colossae from their native son, Epaphras, and let them know of his good works: "Epaphras also says hello. He is a servant of Jesus Christ. And he is from your group. He always prays for you. He prays that you will grow to be spiritually mature *(perfect)* and have everything that God wants for you. I know that he has worked hard for you and the people in Laodicea and in Hierapolis" (Colossians 4:12,13, ERV).

C. We can go always to the life of Jesus Christ for our ultimate example as we try to be like Him. His was a constant example of dedication to His divine purpose and zeal for its accomplishment.

1. We are not told just how He became aware of His divine mission. We are told that He grew in wisdom and stature, and in favour with God and man (Luke 2:52). The Easy-to-Read Version makes this easy for anyone to understand: "Jesus continued to learn more and more. He grew taller. People liked Jesus, and he pleased God."

We are confident that He was aware of God as His Heavenly Father when He went with His parents to Jerusalem at the age of 12. He must have felt so much at home in the temple that He forgot for a time His earthly ties. When His frantic parents found Him after searching for Him for three days, they were amazed when they found Him sitting with the teachers, listening to them and asking questions.

"Son, why have you treated us so? Behold, your father and I have been looking for you anxiously," his mother demanded.

And He said to them, "How is it that you sought me? Did you not know that I must be in my Father's house?" (Luke 2:48,49, RSV). Some translations say, "Wist ye not that I must be about my Father's business?" (KJ).

Although He realized something of His divine purpose, He set a good example for young people. He returned with them to Nazareth and was obedient to them. Although both Mary and Joseph had been given revelations of His unique relationship to God, we are told they did not understand what He had said to them. But like any good mother, Mary treasured those things in her heart.

2. Early in His personal ministry, Jesus demonstrated His dedication to the work God had sent Him to perform. In the second chapter of the Book of John, we are told of the demonstration of His power in turning water into wine. He then went up into the temple, where He found those who were in the temple selling oxen and sheep; there were others with tables set up for the purpose of exchanging money. Many people made long trips on foot to worship at Jerusalem, and this custom may have originated "as a convenience" for them to buy what they needed for required sacrifices. Evidently, though, what had begun as a legitimate service had deteriorated into irreverent practices and fraud. Jesus became a man of action:

And he made a scourge of cords, and drove them all out of the temple, with the sheep and the oxen; and he poured out the coins of the moneychangers, and overturned their tables; and to those who were selling the doves he said, "Take these things away; stop making my Father's house a house of merchandise."

His disciples remembered that it was written, "ZEAL FOR THY HOUSE WILL CONSUME ME" (Psalm 69:9).

The Jews therefore answered and said to him, "What sign do you show to us, seeing that you do these things?"

Jesus answered and said to them, "Destroy this temple, and in

103

three days I will raise it up."

The Jews therefore said, "It took forty-six years to build this temple, and will you raise it up in three days?"

But he was speaking of the temple of his body. When therefore he was raised from the dead, his disciples remembered that he said this; and they believed the scripture, and the word which Jesus had spoken (John 2:15-22, NASV).

3. Jesus continued to be zealous in His Father's business throughout His ministry. He recognized in a blind man an opportunity to further His cause. The disciples had asked whether the man was blind because of his own sin or that of his parents. Jesus replied, "It was not that this man sinned, or his parents, but that the works of God might be made manifest in him. We must work the works of him who sent me, while it is day; night comes, when no one can work. As long as I am in the world, I am the light of the world" (John 9:3,4, RSV). Having said this, Jesus proceeded to anoint the blind man's eyes and instructed him to wash. He obeyed and was relieve of his blindness.

4. While our good works do not save us, it was to prepare a group eager to do good that Jesus became a sacrifice for us. After giving directions to disciples of all ages so that their behavior would not discredit God's Word, but rather would adorn the doctrine, Paul continued his letter to Titus:

For the grace of God has appeared for the salvation of all men, training us to renounce irreligion and worldly passions, and to live sober, upright, and godly lives in this world, awaiting our blessed hope, the appearing of the glory of our great God and Savior Jesus Christ, who gave himself for us to redeem us from all iniquity and to purify for himself a people of his own who are zealous for good deeds (Titus 2:11-14, RSV).

II. Through the miraculous ability of television, we are privileged quite often to see the glow of satisfaction and pride on the face of an Olympic athlete as he hears the strains of his national anthem while his country's flag is above others being raised ceremoniously. This approximates the tremendous triumph felt by one who has been trained, redeemed, and purified by God's grace through Jesus Christ. As she makes every effort to grow in grace and knowledge, she will be zealous of good works, aglow with the Spirit.

A. It is interesting to note the various translations of Romans 12:11b. Each is an attempt to express the burning desire of a dedicated child of God to please his Lord by doing all in his power to manifest his love through obedience and good deeds. The King James says, "fervent in spirit"; the Revised Standard, "aglow with the spirit"; Phillips, "let us keep the fires of the spirit burning"; the New English, "in ardour of spirit"; the Easy-to-Read Version, "be spiritually excited about serving him"; and the Simple English Bible, "serve the Lord with a boiling spirit." I doubt that we will find a better example of letting the various translations define a word or phrase. I don't believe that Webster could have done better!

B. We are to be transformed by the renewing of our minds. Then we are to transmit the light of life. In the beginning God said, "Let there be light!" And there was light! John says, "God is light, and in him there is no darkness at all. If we say we have fellowship with him and yet walk in the darkness, we lie and do not practice the truth; but if we walk in the light as he himself is in the light, we have fellowship with one another, and the blood of Jesus his Son cleanses us from all sin" (1 John 1:5b-7, NASV).

1. Jesus brought heaven's light to earth; it is in His body that we walk in the light, have fellowship one with another. He reflects God's light, making it possible for us to look with confidence toward a light so bright, coming from God, that the Israelites were overwhelmed by its radiance shining from Moses' face. Hence, when Moses returned after speaking with the Lord, he veiled his face. Once Jesus told Thomas, "If you have seen me, you have seen the Father." We see God's light in Christ: "The Son is the shining brightness of God's real being" (Hebrews 1:3, SEB).

Jesus said, "I am the light of the world. The person who follows me will never live in darkness. That person will have the light that gives life" (John 8:12, ERV).

2. We also have the light brought to us through the work of the Holy Spirit in the inspired word of God. The writer of Hebrews says that at one time, God spoke to the fathers in various ways, but in these last days He has spoken through His son. We have the words and teaching of Jesus recorded in the scriptures. Peter heard the voice from heaven on the mountain of transfiguration declaring, "This is my beloved Son, with whom I am well pleased." Peter then says:

> We heard this voice borne from heaven, for we were with him on the holy mountain. And we have the prophetic word made more sure. You will do well to pay attention to this as to a lamp shining in a dark place, until the day dawns and the morning star rises in your hearts. First of all you must understand this, that no prophecy of scripture is a matter of one's own interpretation, because no prophecy ever came by the impulse of man,

but men moved by the Holy Spirit spoke from God" (2 Peter 1:18-21, RSV).

3. Through those inspired words, we are told over and over just what is involved in the process of purifying for Jesus a people zealous of good works; and it is implied—yes, declared—that our souls must be purified through obedience to the truth before our works are acceptable. Thus, we become children of light. Paul contrasts the life of darkness and that of light in several places, among them Ephesians 4 and 5. We have read his admonition: "Put off your old nature which belongs to your former manner of life and is corrupt through deceitful lusts, and be renewed in the spirit of your minds, and put on the new nature, created after the likeness of God in true righteousness and holiness" (Ephesians 4:22-24, RSV). He concludes in the next chapter:

> Therefore be imitators of God, as beloved children. And walk in love, as Christ loved us and gave himself up for us, a fragrant offering and sacrifice to God.
>
> But immorality and all impurity or covetousness must not even be named among you, as is fitting among saints. Let there be no filthiness, nor silly talk, nor levity, which are not fitting; but instead let there be thanksgiving. Be sure of this, that no immoral or impure man, or one who is covetous (that is, an idolator), has any inheritance in the kingdom of Christ and of God. Let no one deceive you with empty words, for it is because of these things that the wrath of God comes upon the sons of disobedience. Therefore, do not associate with them, for once you were darkness, but now you are light in the Lord; walk as children of light (for the fruit of light is found in all that is good and right and true), and try to learn what is pleasing to the Lord (Ephesians 5:1-10, RSV).

Remember that Jesus commanded that we let our light shine before men, that they may see our good works and glorify God. Paul again emphasizes that Christians must be good examples to the world: "Do all things without grumbling or disputing; that you may prove yourselves to be blameless and innocent, children of God above reproach in the midst of a crooked and perverse generation, among whom you appear as light in the world, holding fast the word of life" (Philippians 2:14-16a, NASV).

If we are to light our little corner of the world, we Christians **must** be "aglow with the Spirit"!

III. Christians radiating the fruit of light—all that is right and good and true—will be busy serving the Lord. They were spoken by

106

Moses to the children of Israel, but in principle we can apply these instructions to our lives today: "And now, Israel, what does the Lord your God require from you, but to fear the Lord your God, to walk in all His ways and love Him, and to serve the Lord your God with all your heart and with all your soul, and to keep the Lord's commandments and his statutes which I command you today for your good? (Deuteronomy 10:12,13, NASV).

Our commandments under Christ as our head are different; we have been freed from laws given only to the Israelites when we, as Gentiles, were outside that law. In Paul's writings, we see plainly that both Jews and Gentiles are one in Christ's body, the church. However, as we approach God through Christ, we are to come before Him in reverence. We are to obey the commandments given us in the New Testament, which include loving God with all our hearts, souls, and strength. We must be totally committed to His service as living sacrifices.

A. From the beginning of His ministry, Jesus emphasized the necessity of worshiping, serving, and obeying God. He rebuffed Satan's offer of all of the kingdoms of the world in exchange for Satan worship with a quotation from scripture: "Go away, Satan, because it is written: 'You must worship the Lord your God. Serve only Him' " (Matthew 4:10, SEB). In His sermon on the mount, Jesus outlined the new values of His kingdom. He showed that His ministry was to fulfill the law and would surpass it in emphasizing sincerity of service rather than outward forms. He emphasized trust and obedience to God, concluding that merely claiming Jesus as Lord would not supplant obedience to God's will.

B. There is no reason to attempt in this study to cover all of the avenues of service to God covered in the New Testament. There really is no excuse for anyone to take my word or that of any person to understand the scope of our service to God. We have a relatively short volume including the 27 books of the New Testament. It takes much less time to read it through than we spend in reading a popular novel or some government instructions we are to obey. In most of the epistles written by Paul, we find encouragement and direction in acceptable, practical Christianity. As we maintain Christian homes in a world where we see Satan using all kinds of means to destroy this basic unit of society, we are serving the Lord. There is service to be rendered to the poor, to strangers, in fellowship and worship, to the community, the government, and especially to widows and orphans. But we must never forget that in being subject to one another and fulfilling our roles as family members, we are serving the Lord!

Paul is very clear in his instruction to members of a family:

107

Let each one of you love his wife as himself, and let the wife see that she respects her husband. Children, obey your parents in the Lord, for this is right. "Honor your father and mother" (this is the first commandment with a promise), "that it may be well with you and that you may live long on the earth." Fathers, do not provoke your children to anger, but bring them up in the discipline and instruction of the Lord.

Slaves, be obedient to those who are your earthly masters, with fear and trembling, in singleness of heart, as to Christ: not in the way of eye-service, as men-pleasers, but as servants of Christ, doing the will of God from the heart, rendering service with a good will as to the Lord and not to men, knowing that whatever good any one does, he will receive the same again from the Lord, whether he is a slave or free. Masters, do the same to them, and forbear threatening, knowing that he who is both their Master and yours is in heaven, and that there is no partiality with him. Finally, be strong in the Lord and in the strength of his might (Ephesians 5:33 – 6:1-10, RSV).

In this passage, we see the instruction extending outside the home to the employer-employee relationship as we know it today. There is, from the Christian view, a triangle dimension to each relationship: person A, person B, and Christ—whether it be husband and wife, father or mother and child, or employer and employee. Our focus is on heaven while serving on earth. Our aim as we serve is to give God the glory.

Conclusion: In view of God's gracious love and the tremendous sacrifice of Jesus Christ, we accept thankfully the privilege of being children of God, children of light. Kingdoms of earth rise and fall, come and go, but we are members of the kingdom, the church of Christ. Jesus promised that the gates of hell would not prevail against it. We follow the example of Jesus and His disciples in rendering zealous service to God. Unlike the Israelites, forbidden to approach Mount Sinai where God met with Moses, we have come to an everlasting kingdom:

But you have come to Mount Zion and to the city of the living God, the heavenly Jerusalem, and to myriads of angels, to the general assembly and church of the firstborn who are enrolled in heaven, and to God, the judge of all, and to the spirits of righteous men made perfect, and to Jesus, the mediator of a new covenant, and to the sprinkled blood, which speaks better than the blood of Abel. See to it that you do not refuse him who is speaking. For if those did not escape when they refused him who warned them on earth, much less shall we escape who turn away from him who warns from heaven. And his voice shook the earth then, but now he has promised, saying, "YET ONCE MORE I WILL SHAKE NOT ONLY THE EARTH, BUT ALSO THE HEAVEN."

And this expression, "yet once more," denotes the removing of those things which can be shaken, as of created things, in order that those things which cannot be shaken may remain.

Therefore, since we receive a kingdom which cannot be shaken, let us show gratitude, by which we may offer to God an acceptable service with reverence and awe (Hebrews 12:22-28, NASV).

Through God's power working in us, Christ who strengthens us, and the guidance provided by the Holy Spirit through the scriptures, may we "never flag in zeal, be aglow with the Spirit, serve the Lord" (Romans 12:11, RSV).

Daily Bible Reading

Sunday
Christian Behavior
(Romans 12)

Monday
Righteous Zeal
(Psalm 119:137-144)

Tuesday
Paul's Zealous Example
(1 Thessalonians 2:1-12)

Wednesday
A People Zealous of Good Works
(Titus 2)

Thursday
Be Zealous to Make It Sure
(2 Peter 1)

Friday
Walk in the Light
(1 John 1)

Saturday
Be Imitators of God
(Ephesians 5 and 6)

Memory Verses

Romans 12:9-11

Chapter 10

Hope, Patience, and Prayer

Introduction: As a Christian, you have something very valuable which no woman of the world can have, however clean and moral her life may be. Your faith, produced by hearing the gospel, has led you to an obedience which placed you in the body of Christ, His church. You have a lively hope that prompts you to look for strength from above to help you overcome trials along your way. Like Moses, you look beyond the immediate to the ultimate goal:

> By faith, when Moses had grown up, he said no to being called "Pharaoh's daughter's son." God's people were being mistreated. Moses chose to be mistreated also, instead of having fun for a while doing sinful things. SUFFERING shame for the Messiah was more important to Moses than the rich treasures of Egypt. He was looking ahead to the reward (Hebrews 11:24-26, SEB).

Your happiness is not based on the circumstance of the day; rather, you rejoice in the hope you have in Christ Jesus. You do not give up when trials come your way. Because of God's limitless power working in you, depression cannot darken your sky. Through Christ, you can talk to your heavenly Father about your troubles, and you utter prayers of thanks daily for the blessings you receive. Should you ever reach the point where you are unable to word an acceptable prayer, you are reminded that you have the help of the Holy Spirit. Paul's admonition is not just a command to be obeyed; it is a sure guideline to a successful life, an eternal reward: "Rejoice in your hope, be patient in tribulation, be constant in prayer" (Romans 12:12, RSV).

I. Christ **in you** brings with Him the hope of all the wonderful things to come. Here resides your hope of glory. We have access today to so many instances of glorious achievement. Young athletes begin training at an early age, even move away from home so that the training can be more intense. They get tired. They get homesick. They get hungry. Why do they do it? They are weary in body but rejoicing in the hope of being the best in the world in their event. That is their hope of glory.

When you give up many things pertaining to a life of sin, determine to present your body a living sacrifice to God, why do you do it? Your reason is very similar to that of the athlete—you have a vision of the glory that is to come to you. For the same reason, Paul was able to forego the honor which surely would have been his as an accomplished Jew of the strictest sect, and to suffer many hardships for the sake of Christ, whom he had persecuted:

> I am happy in my sufferings for you. There are many things that Christ must still suffer through his body, the church. I am accepting my part of these things that must be suffered. I accept these sufferings in my body. I suffer for his body, the church. I became a servant of the church because God gave me a special work to do. This work helps you. My work is to tell fully the teaching of God. This teaching is the secret truth that was hidden since the beginning of time. This truth was hidden from all people. But now that secret truth is made known to God's people. God decided to let his people know that rich and glorious truth. That truth is for all people. That truth is Christ himself, who is in you. He is our only hope for glory . . . You were raised from death with Christ . . . Your old sinful self has died, and your new life is kept with Christ in God. Christ is your life. When he comes again, you will share in his glory (Colossians 1:24-27; 3:1a,3,4; ERV).

Not all the glory is in the future. It is a real blessing to know that our lives are kept with Christ in God. Christ is our life. In one chapter, John recorded the promise that the Holy Spirit, Christ, and God will dwell in the believer, the one who loves Christ and keeps His Word: "If you love me, you will keep my commandments. And I will pray the Father, and he will give you another Counselor, to be with you for ever, even the Spirit of truth, whom the world cannot receive, because it neither sees him nor knows him; you know him, for he dwells in you, and will be in you" (John 14:15-17, RSV).

One of the disciples, hearing the discussion recorded in this chapter, asked Jesus how He was going to manifest Himself to them but not to the world. Jesus answered him, "If a man loves me, he will keep my word, and my Father will love him, and we will come to him and make our home with him" (John 14:23, RSV).

If the president of the United States came and spent one night at your house, you probably would be the envy of the town. All the world would hear through the newspapers and magazines, and perhaps see on television, just how you were honored by the visit of such an important man. True, the world does not see—perhaps cannot see—God, Christ, and the Holy Spirit living in us—not physically, anyway. But as we bear the fruit of the Spirit, they can see the result of our daily walk with the Trinity—immeasurably more important, more glorious than any man who ever lived!

A. We grieve for those who do not share this glorious hope. It is true that at one time, the Gentiles were without hope: "Therefore remember that you Gentiles in the flesh . . . were at that time separated from Christ, alienated from the commonwealth of Israel, and strangers to the covenants of promise, having no hope and without God in the world" (Ephesians 2:11a,12b, RSV). We must keep reminding ourselves that the law of Moses was given to the Jews only; others, unless they become proselytes, were not included. We are thankful, though, as Paul reminds us in so much of his writing, that they can obey the gospel and become heirs of the hope extended to all mankind in Christ.

Those who do not obey the gospel remain without hope. The Christian's hope provides comfort in this life which extends beyond death. Paul discussed the resurrection from the dead, explaining that the dead in Christ would rise first at Christ's second coming; then those who were alive would be caught up to meet them in the air. He introduced the discussion by stating his purpose: "That you may not grieve as others do who have no hope" (1 Thessalonians 4:13c). In 2 Thessalonians 1:8,9, he shows that those who do not accept and follow the teachings of the gospel will suffer God's righteous judgment—eternal destruction and exclusion from the presence of God.

B. For you as a Christian, the sinner's hopelessness is replaced by a life full of hope, sustained by your knowledge of the great and precious promises made to those who love the Savior. Not all of the promises pertain to life after death. I have heard men boast of the brotherhood they experience in a lodge, but that really cannot compare to the worldwide fellowship of brothers and sisters in Christ. Back in the days when there was great prejudice in many places against association with black people, we had a beloved sister in Christ from Jamaica spend a few days with us. Her son, a professional man in New York, chided her, "You certainly are a brave woman taking a bus tour through Texas, stopping to visit there!" Her confident reply was, "I have Christian friends in Texas."

In addition to the earthly joys in our new life, we do look forward to our eternal inheritance in heaven. We should join Peter in his expression of gratitude for these blessings: "Praise be to God and Father of our

Lord Jesus Christ. God has great mercy, and because of his mercy he gave us a new life. This new life brings us a living hope through Jesus Christ's rising from death. Now we hope for the blessings God has for his children. Those blessings are kept for you in heaven. Those blessings cannot ruin or be destroyed or lose their beauty. God's power protects you through your faith and it keeps you safe until your salvation comes. That salvation is ready to be given to you at the end of time" (1 Peter 1:3-5, ERV).

C. We can be encouraged to go on hoping as we read of those in Old Testament times who were helped by God to endure their many trials. Just think how God traveled with the murmuring, complaining Israelites during their wilderness wanderings. We cannot expect Him to appear to or lead us with a cloud by day and a pillar of fire by night, but we have always with us the scriptures which can give us assurance and guidance as we travel the narrow way: "For whatever was written in earlier times was written for our instruction, that through perseverance and the encouragement of the scriptures we might have hope (Romans 15:4, NASV).

You will remember that Paul spent several chapters in the first part of Romans showing that both Jew and Gentile have equal access to the salvation for which Jesus Christ gave Himself as the final sacrifice. As he concludes the epistle, he turns to the scriptures to show that the Christ became a servant to the circumcision to confirm the promise made to the patriarchs. He quotes prophecies to confirm that through "the root of Jesse" the Gentiles, too, would have the hope of salvation. You recall, of course, that Jesse was the father of David, and Christ came through the lineage of David. Forgetting our ancestry, we all can experience together a radiant hope, overflowing to God's glory: "I pray that the God who gives hope will fill you with much joy and peace while you trust in him. Then you will be full of hope and it will flow out of you by the power of the Holy Spirit" (Romans 15:13, ERV).

II. When tribulations or trials come—and come they will—we are encouraged to stand firm, persevere, endure with patience. It takes practically no effort to drift with the tide, to enjoy calm waters and blue skies. Those who are strong will grow in character as they develop patience by facing and overcoming tribulations. Peter tells us to cast our cares on the Lord, for He cares for us (1 Peter 5:7). As we are comforted, we can comfort others.

Paul recognized God as our source of comfort:

Blessed be the God and Father of our Lord Jesus Christ, the Father of mercies and God of all comfort, who comforts us in all our affliction, so that we may be able to comfort those who are in

114

any affliction, with the comfort with which we ourselves are comforted by God. For as we share abundantly in Christ's sufferings, so through Christ we share abundantly in comfort too. If we are afflicted, it is for your comfort and salvation; and if we are comforted it is for your comfort, which you experience when you patiently endure the same sufferings that we suffer (2 Corinthians 1:3-6, RSV).

A. Patience is necessary if we are to receive our reward. One who is patient has learned to endure trials or aggravation without complaint. It is perhaps one of the qualities most needed by mothers of young children. They may be able to meet crises daily, but putting up with spilled milk, scattered toys, and siblings' bickering may get them down. I remember one lovely young mother who confided, "I started today by praying that the Lord would help me develop patience, and he has given me plenty of practice. I never had so many little things go wrong!" We all have heard, no doubt, of someone who prayed, "Lord, give me patience, and give it to me **now**!"

The Hebrew Christians were encouraged with these words: "Remember those days when you first learned the truth. You had a hard struggle with many sufferings, but you continued strong. Sometimes people said hateful things to you and persecuted you before many people . . . And you still had joy when all the things you owned were taken away from you. You continued with joy because you knew that you had something much better that would continue forever. So don't lose the courage that you had in the past. Your courage will be rewarded richly. You must be patient. After you have done what God wants, then you will get the things that he promised you" (Hebrews 10:32,33a,34b-36, ERV).

1. Patience is one of the qualities included in what we call "the Christian graces." Peter declares that we have God's great and precious promises through which we can escape the corruption that is in the world and become **partakers of the divine nature**! What a privilege! We surely should, then, be willing to work diligently to add to our faith virtue, knowledge, temperance, **patience**, godliness, brotherly kindness, and love.

2. In our patience, we demonstrate our maturity. You would be insulted if someone called you "childish." Each of us can remember when we wanted more than anything else to be grown-up. That may have been partially because we wanted the privileges enjoyed by our older brothers and sisters, but it still was a goal we set for ourselves. Patience is one of the attributes older men should possess, according to Paul's instruction to the young preacher Titus. He wrote,

"Teach the older men to have self-control, to be serious, and to be wise. They should be strong in the faith, strong in love, and strong in patience" (Titus 2:2, ERV). Older women, also, were to include these qualities in their holy lives as they taught the younger women.

3. Happiness is not just having lots of fun or having all the things we want. True happiness comes from being able to meet life's challenges successfully. There may be times when you want to throw up your hands and quit when faced with your adolescent's antics. But how you glow with pride when she is elected class president, is named to the honor society, and walks across the stage to receive her diploma. Or you may be just as proud when one who is not a natural leader or scholar passes that dreaded test and goes on to graduation. The exercise of our patience leads toward perfection; we actually can find pleasure in overcoming the obstacles between us and our goal: "My brothers and sisters, you will have many kinds of troubles. But when these things happen, you should be very happy. Why? Because you know that these things are testing your faith. And this will give you patience. Let your patience make you stronger and stronger. Then you will be perfect. You will have everything you need" (James 1:2-4, ERV).

B. Our children learn much by following in our footsteps. Whether that learning is good or bad depends on the direction we are going. Do you lead them into activities or places where they may be tempted to sin, or do you provide the wise guidance and example that will assure their walking in the "strait and narrow way that leads to life" (Matthew 7:13,14, KJ)? If I am able to say, "Follow me as I follow Christ," you may follow me with confidence!

So much in our ability to be patient in tribulation depends on our attitude. Because His life was focused on the purpose for which He came to earth and the eventual joy of being reunited with His Father in heaven, Jesus was able to bear all the suffering, trials, and indignity heaped upon Him:

> We must put aside anything that might slow us down. Sin can easily tie us up. Let us run with endurance the race that is ahead of us. Jesus endured when he had to suffer shame and die on a cross. Why? Because of the happiness that lay ahead for him. He didn't mind the way he had to die.
>
> Keep your eyes on Jesus. He is the beginning and the goal of our faith. Now he sits at the right side of God's throne. Think about what Jesus had to endure from sinners—they were all against him. Then you will not get tired and give up (Hebrews 12:1b-3, SEB).

116

C. The person who said that there's nothing in a name was entirely wrong! (Just try writing the name of another person on a check!) We are honored to wear the name of a godly parent even if others criticize or persecute him. Thousands of patriots have given their lives because they were proud to be called "Americans." How much greater is our privilege of being members of God's family, called by the name of His son! For this reason, we can be patient as we endure trials, looking forward to sharing in His triumph:

> Beloved, do not be surprised at the fiery ordeal which comes upon you to prove you, as though something strange were happening to you. But rejoice in so far as you share Christ's sufferings, that you may also rejoice and be glad when his glory is revealed. If you are reproached for the name of Christ, you are blessed, because the spirit of glory and of God rests upon you. But let none of you suffer as a murderer, or a thief, or a wrongdoer, or a mischief-maker; yet if one suffers as a Christian, let him not be ashamed, but under that name let him glorify God (1 Peter 4:12-16, RSV).

III. Ours is an age of communication. Most of you have grown up in an age when it is taken for granted that we can, literally, hear instantly words spoken anywhere on our globe. Yet we see families drifting apart because they have lost the art of communication. They are unable to convey to those closest to them the things that trouble them or make them happy. Often this communication gap can be closed through the help of a trusted counselor, perhaps an older and wiser family member. We may marvel at our access to electronic communication and rejoice at the power to heal afforded by simply talking to each other. But we always have had access to a means of communication more powerful than the president's hot line to our country's enemies or friends—it is called **prayer**!

What a blessing it is that we can talk to God as our Heavenly Father—that Jesus, who has been tempted in every way that we are tempted and truly understands, will intercede with the Father for us; also, that we have the help of the Holy Spirit in making our communication effective. God's ears are open to those who, by obedience to His commands, keep the lines of communication open. It is hard to imagine that we would need Paul's admonition to be "instant in prayer" (Romans 12:12c, KJ).

We get a sense of the urgency of being faithful in prayer as we look at various translations of this short passage. We learn that in addition to being faithful in the exercise of this privilege, we are to be devoted, constant, make prayer a habit, continual, and persistent. Paul admonished,

"Pray without ceasing" (1 Thessalonians 5:17, KJ).

A. Does this mean that we are to be muttering a prayer all the time, or does it mean that we are always to be in a prayerful mood? If you skip a meal, have you ceased to eat? No, we understand that only those who are on a hunger strike have ceased to eat. One of the greatest obstacles to the dieter, too, is to be constantly in the mood to eat! From the abundance of material on good nutrition available, we have learned that we best serve the physical needs of our bodies when we eat sensibly and regularly.

In the same way, we take advantage of the information available to us in God's Word and in many books and pamphlets to help us pray to God in a manner acceptable to God and fruitful to our spiritual growth. Our purpose in this discussion is not to do a deep study on prayer, but to emphasize the necessity of our taking advantage of the privilege of private prayer. You may want to read again our study of both private and corporate prayer in my book *The Wise Woman Builds Her House*, Chapter VIII, beginning on page 89. In God's Word, we do have all the information we need to avoid those things which would hinder our prayers and to pray successfully.

1. Jesus used a parable to teach the necessity of persistent prayer:

> Then Jesus taught the followers that they should always pray and never lose hope. Jesus used this story to teach them: "Once there was a judge in a town. He did not care about God. The judge also did not care what people thought about him. In that same town there was a woman. Her husband was dead. The woman came many times to this judge and said, 'There is a man who is doing bad things to me. Give me my rights!' But the judge did not want to help the woman. After a long time, the judge thought to himself, 'I don't care about God. And I don't care about what people think. But this woman is bothering me. If I give her what she wants, then she will leave me alone. But if I don't give her what she wants, she will bother me until I am sick!' "
>
> The Lord (*Jesus*) said, "Listen! **There is meaning** in what the bad judge said. God's people shout to him night and day. God will always give his people what is right. God will not be slow to answer his people. I tell you, God will help his people quickly! (Luke 18:1-8a, ERV).

2. Prayer will help us to resist all the devil's methods of attack. First, we must put on the Christian's armour: truth, righteousness, the gospel of peace, the shield of faith, the helmet of salvation, and the sword of the Spirit, which is the word of God. Paul concludes

118

his admonition for the Christian to put on the whole armour of God by saying, "Pray at all times in the Spirit, with all prayer and supplication. To that end keep alert with all perseverance, making supplication for all the saints" (Ephesians 6:18, RSV).

3. Often we hear a man pray from the pulpit that the preacher may recall easily the lesson he has prepared. I heard one preacher remark that petition was unnecessary, if not improper, since it was his responsibility to prepare well in order to preach as he should. I realize he was pointing out that our ministers today cannot rely on the Spirit to put the words in their mouths. I appreciate that it is necessary for those of us who assume the awesome responsibility of teaching to prepare well. However, it is never wrong for us to pray that God's power working in us will give us the ability to be effective in our work. Paul, an inspired apostle, not only urged continual prayer, but asked often that he be included in the prayers of the saints:

> Continue steadfastly in prayer, being watchful in it with thanks-giving; and pray for us also, that God may open to us a door for the word, to declare the mystery of Christ, on account of which I am in prison, that I may make it clear, as I ought to speak (Colossians 4:2-4, RSV).

B. We find many examples of fervent, regular habits of prayer among those who served the Lord. Daniel was a young man who had been taken into captivity with his people because of their disobedience. However, he had been trained so well that he won favor from the heathen rulers and became a ruler over many of his captors. This provoked jealousy among the natives who wanted to discredit him but could find no fault in his character. They devised a scheme, though, to have him thrown into the lions' den. Pretending to honor the king, they appealed to his vanity by suggesting that an irrevocable law, according to the laws of the Medes and Persians, be proclaimed that anyone who prayed during the next 30 days to any god or man other than the king be thrown to the lions.

Daniel was aware of the decree, but he went as was his custom to his upstairs room, where the windows opened toward Jerusalem. He got down on his knees three times a day and prayed, giving thanks to God.

With what glee Daniel's accusers went to the king, demanding that the decree be carried out. The king knew Daniel's character and, also, that he was trustworthy and neither corrupt nor negligent. He did everything in his power to save Daniel but finally, when he had to carry out the law, he prayed that the God whom Daniel had served so faithfully would rescue him. After spending a sleepless night, the king hurried to the lions' den and was overjoyed to find that Daniel was not harmed

119

because he had trusted in his God. He commanded that Daniel's accusers be thrown into the lions' den, then proclaimed throughout the land that all people must fear and reverence the God of Daniel (Daniel 6).

At times, we may wonder why we should keep expressing our needs to God in prayer; He knows what we need. Jesus emphasized that He and God were one, yet He prayed to God often. Jesus spent a busy evening at the home of Simon and Andrew, where He healed Simon's mother-in-law, then spent the rest of the day healing the sick and demon-possessed among the throng who gathered at the door. We're not told when He went to bed, but very early the following morning, while it was still dark, He got up, left the house, and went to a solitary place to pray (Mark 1:29-35).

When Jesus' ministry became so hectic that He and the disciples hardly had time to eat, He cautioned them to withdraw from the crowds and get some rest. Later, after feeding the 5,000, He had the disciples get into a boat and go on ahead of Him while He dismissed the crowd. He then went into the hills to pray (Mark 6:30-46).

Earlier in His ministry, Jesus spent the whole night praying. He had been performing miracles, healing people, and gathering a following of disciples. He was aware of the work He came to do and of the prophecies he would fulfill. When morning came, He called His disciples to Him and appointed the 12 apostles who would be His companions and co-workers for approximately three years. As people came to hear Him speak, He took the apostles with Him to a level place on the mountain, and there He delivered the "magna carta," the guiding principles of His gospel, which we know as the "Sermon on the Mount" (Luke 6:12-16ff.).

Although we have a few of the prayers of Jesus recorded, the one known by the world as "The Lord's Prayer" is actually a model prayer He gave as an example to His disciples. In John 17, the entire chapter, we have His longest recorded prayer. He knew He was to be betrayed by one of the 12 that very night and that He would endure a mock trial and then be crucified. But it was not for Himself he prayed, but for His disciples—both those who were with Him then and those who would believe later because of their teaching. He prayed for all of us who profess His name!

It was in the Garden of Gethsemane that He prayed His most passionate prayer—this one for Himself. However, He never forgot His divine mission, but prayed only that His cup of suffering be removed. Even then, with His sweat falling like drops of blood, He prayed, "Yet not my will, but yours be done" (Luke 22:39-45).

The early Christians followed their Lord's example in prayer. When Peter was thrown in prison, the church gathered at the house of Mary, the mother of John Mark, where fervent prayers were offered for Peter. They still were praying when Peter, who had been led out of prison by an angel, knocked on the door. We may be slightly amused at their reaction when they saw Peter standing there. Their prayer had been answered, but at first they did not believe that it was Peter. Then, when they saw him, they were amazed. Are we amazed—fail to be thankful—when our prayers are answered?

When Paul and Silas were thrown into the most secure prison in Philippi, they not only spent their time praying but also in singing praise to God. The answer to their prayers was truly earthshaking. An earthquake caused the foundations of the prison to be shaken, and immediately all the doors were opened, and everyone's chains were unfastened. Paul and Silas answered the frightened jailer's question—"Sirs, what must I do to be saved?"—by preaching Jesus Christ to him and his household. He and his household were baptized into Christ and probably became the backbone of the Philippian church, which did so much to support Paul in his ministry.

Conclusion: Christians are the happiest people in the world because of their hope in Christ. They meet tribulation joyfully because their eyes are fixed on the author and finisher of their faith; they wait with patience for His coming again, when they can claim their eternal reward. They are grateful that they can go directly to their Heavenly Father in prayer, through Jesus Christ, their mediator. They pray all the time!

Daily Bible Reading

Sunday

Examples of Faith
(Hebrews 11)

Monday

Christ, Our Hope
(Colossians 1:3-28)

Tuesday

Without Hope
(Ephesians 2:11,12; 1 Thessalonians 4:13;
2 Thessalonians 1:8,9)

Wednesday

A Living Hope
(1 Peter 1:3-25)

Thursday

God Helps Us Overcome Troubles
(2 Corinthians 1:3-11)

Friday

Patient in Troubles
(1 Peter 4:1-19)

Saturday

Christ's Prayer for Us
(John 17)

Memory Verses

1 Peter 1:3-5

Colossians 4:2

Chapter 11

Practice Hospitality

Introduction: The home of an elder and his wife was overflowing with guests who were attending a lectureship. One of them complimented him on his hospitality. Without hesitation he replied, "All that we have is the Lord's. This is his house. I must use it for him!"

How often do we say, "**My** house, money, car, even child?" They **all** belong to the Lord. He has loaned them to us and we, as stewards, must give an account of their use. May we be able to do it with joy!

David said, "The earth is the Lord's, and the fulness thereof; the world, and they that dwell therein" (Psalm 24:1, KJ).

Paul concludes a paragraph beginning with "Let love be genuine" with the admonition, "Contribute to the needs of the saints, practice hospitality" (Romans 12:13, RSV).

Our love for the Lord overflows to our brothers and sisters in Christ. If they are in need, we share with them what the Lord has entrusted to us. They always are welcome in our homes, whether or not they have physical needs. We use our homes to entertain strangers because, in so doing, we may be entertaining angels.

I. Paul definitely is not asking us to contribute to the needs of a person who, after his death, has been declared by some council to be a saint. Every Christian is a saint, made so by a power much higher than any earthly conference. Since we saints are children of God, we also are members of one family. We show our brotherly affection, then, by our generosity in ministering to the needs of the saints.

A. On more than one occasion, Jesus taught generosity. He indicated that God's giving to us is based on our giving to others: "Give to other people, and you will receive. You will be given much. It will be poured into your hands—more than you can hold. You will be given so much that it will spill into your lap. The way you give to other people is the way God will give to you" (Luke 6:38, ERV).

His concern was for our own attitude and well-being, perhaps, as much as for the good our gifts would bestow on others. We have noted that He warned we cannot serve both God and money, that we must not trust in our riches. At one time Jesus said, "Sell the things you have and give that money to people who need it. The riches of this world don't continue. So get the kind of riches that continue. Get the treasure of heaven. That treasure continues forever. Thieves can't steal your treasure in heaven, and moths can't destroy it. Your heart will be where your treasure is" (Luke 12:33,34, ERV).

B. In his farewell address to the Ephesian elders, Paul reminded them of his own example of industry and sharing: "You yourselves know that these hands ministered to my necessities, and to those who were with me. In all things I have shown you that by so toiling one must help the weak, remembering the words of the Lord Jesus, how he said, 'It is more blessed to give than to receive' " (Acts 20:34,35, RSV).

It actually is easier to give than to receive. You have known the satisfaction of making another happy by giving something which was needed or desired. If you have not felt, you have known through others the humiliation—even pain—of having to ask for help. That is one reason we need to be sensitive to the needs of our fellow Christians. God expects us also to be generous in meeting those needs.

James uses failure to minister to the needs we see as an illustration of faith without works:

> *What does it profit, my brethren, if a man says he has faith but has no works? Can his faith save him? If a brother or sister is illclad and in lack of daily food, and one of you says to them, "Go in peace, be warmed and filled," without giving them the things needed for the body, what does it profit? So faith by itself, if it has no works, is dead (James 2:14-17, RSV).*

C. The love which guides us in ministering to the needy should, however, be **agape**, the love that is mindful of the good of the recipient. Neither Jesus nor Paul expected people who were able to work to depend on others for a living. Countless stories other than in scripture illustrate the fact that a person or an animal whose needs come too easily becomes weak and dependent. We have seen an illustration of this fact in our own government. Once on welfare, many cease to put forth the effort to be self-supporting. They find it difficult to give up the benefits they receive through welfare for the pride they would have in doing for themselves. Apparently, there were those in Thessalonica who felt the same way. Paul is very explicit in his instruction that this should not be allowed:

In the name of the Lord Jesus Christ, we command you, brothers, to keep away from every brother who is idle and does not live according to the teaching you received from us. For you yourselves know how you ought to follow our example. We were not idle when we were with you, nor did we eat anyone's food without paying for it. On the contrary, we worked night and day, laboring and toiling so that we would not be a burden to any of you. We did this, not because we do not have the right to such help, but in order to make ourselves a model for you to follow. For even when we were with you, we gave you this rule: "If a man will not work, he shall not eat."

We hear that some among you are idle. They are not busy; they are busybodies. Such people we command and urge in the Lord Jesus Christ, to settle down and earn the bread they eat (2 Thessalonians 3:6-12, NIV).

The best approach to helping the able-bodied who are in need is to help them to help themselves. This may be done by counseling, training, or helping to locate jobs they are capable of filling. At times, the most loving answer to their request is a kind but firm "no." Walter Billingsley, overseer of the Christian Service Center in Tulsa, demonstrates the warmhearted but hardheaded agape love needed in many cases. Rather than allowing the greedy to remove from the storerooms loads of the best clothing and supplies given by caring Christians, he instructs his workers to limit the number of items given for each member of a family. By refusing to give household necessities to some person simply wanting but not needing them, he assures a supply on hand to meet the needs of a family suffering a fire or a natural disaster. A planned attempt is made, too, to meet a person's spiritual as well as physical needs. Thus, the Center is contributing, on behalf of all the Christians who help to make it possible, to those in need. Some who were not Christians become members of the Lord's body, numbered among the saints.

II. Practice hospitality! Real Christian hospitality is an extension of the loving care due the saints. It can be a real means of encouraging spiritual growth among the saints and in leading others to become Christians. It is not an activity planned to exhibit our lovely homes and possessions to those who will then return the invitation. While good manners, based on consideration, always are in order, our hospitality should not be a means of parading our social graces.

A. In our hospitality, we are dispensers of God's magnificently varied grace. This is not something we do just because we feel it is a duty, perhaps wishing we didn't have to do it. Just think of all that

God has given us! It is a privilege to be able to share our homes and our food with others. A few decades ago, hospitality flowed between Christians naturally. I remember quite well, back in the 1920s, that we rarely ate a Sunday noon meal alone. One or more of the children brought another home with them. Sometimes it was a whole family. Some waited and played while others ate around the long dining table. We were invited into other homes just as regularly. Today, we have much larger, nicer homes, but the spontaneity seems to have disappeared from our hospitality. Congregations employ various means to encourage us to share our homes and love with one another. We all seem to be so much busier than we were a few decades ago, but we must remember that our hospitality can cement a friendship which can help a new Christian to grow so that he will not become one of the many who fall away.

Hospitality is not something we may or may not choose to practice. We have been taught that we are to obey commandments passed on to us by the inspired writers of the New Testament. We are careful to obey the primary principles which put us into Christ, but are we as careful about those that are important to our relationships as Christians? We have noted Paul's command. Peter is just as specific, even touching on our attitude in our performance:

> The most important thing is loving one another with all your heart, because love covers many, many sins. Invite one another into your homes without complaining about it. Each person should use the **spiritual** gift he has received to help other people, like a good manager of the many kinds of God's gracious love (1 Peter 4:8-10, SEB).

B. The scriptures abound with examples of hospitality. Some entertained fellow Christians; others entertained strangers. In times when there were not so many commercial accommodations for travelers, it was necessary for them to be invited into homes. Even in our pioneer days, doors were left unlocked, and it was not unusual for some weary cowboy to enter a dugout, prepare himself a meal, and take a nap when the owner had driven the long miles to town but left the latchstring out. Just as those Jesus sent out stayed in homes that welcomed them, our pioneer preachers lodged with Christians who repaid their spiritual food with good eating to sustain their bodies. Not all of the spiritual food was dispensed from the pulpit, either. Unbelieving husbands have been won to Christ when they allowed their wives to extend hospitality to a visiting preacher.

1. We may not know the good we may do or the blessing which may come to us as we entertain strangers. Certainly, we incur some danger when we take into our homes those who may be derelict or criminal. But we have many opportunities to show hospitality to fellow Christians who drive or fly many miles to attend workshops or lectureships. In encouraging us to do just that, one elder said, "They are the cream of the crop. You will form lasting friendships." Hundreds of Christians in Tulsa can verify that fact. Some have had as many as 30 in their homes. When the beds and couches are filled, bedrolls occupy every available space. The annual Soul-Winning Workshop is truly a spiritual feast in its program and in the opportunity we have to practice hospitality!

The inspired writer put it so plainly: "You are brothers **and sisters** in Christ, so continue loving each other. Always remember to help people by accepting them into your home. Some people have done that and have helped angels without knowing it" (Hebrews 13:1,2, ERV).

2. Both Abraham and Lot welcomed strangers who actually were angels sent from God. Abraham is known as the father of the faithful because he left his home when the Lord directed him to a country he did not know. For years, he had been expecting God to fulfill His promise of a son who would be the ancestor of the nation he was to be given. When he was 99 years old, he was sitting in the door of his tent in the heat of the day. He looked up to see three men standing opposite him. He ran to meet them and bowed.

"My lord, if now I have found favor in your sight, please do not pass your servant by. Please let a little water be brought and wash your feet, and rest yourselves under the tree; and I will bring a piece of bread, that you may refresh yourselves; after that you may go on, since you have visited your servant," he said. And they said, "So do as you have said."

As they rested, Abraham hurried to ask Sarah to prepare bread while he selected a tender calf to be prepared by a servant. He visited with the strangers while they ate. Then they told him that within a year, Sarah would bear to him the promised son. It was possibly only then that he realized he had, indeed, entertained angels (Genesis 18:1-33, quotes NASV).

Lot, Abraham's nephew who had chosen to live in Sodom, displayed the same hospitality. The Lord had revealed to Abraham that Sodom and Gomorrah were going to be destroyed because of the wickedness of their people. When not even 10 righteous men could be found there, for whom the Lord had promised He would not destroy the place, the two angels went to warn Lot, whose soul was vexed because of the wickedness. When Lot saw them, he rose and bowed with his face to the ground saying, "Now behold, my lords, please turn aside into your servant's house, and spend the night, and wash your feet; then you may rise early and go on your way." They suggested spending the night in the square, but he urged them strongly, and they became his guests. After being threatened by the men of the town, they revealed their identity and the Lord's plan to Lot. When morning came, they hurried Lot and his family out of the town before it was destroyed (Genesis 19:1-22).

3. We see examples of New Testament hospitality in the first two converts in Philippi. Lydia was a businesswoman who had come from Thyatira and was a seller of purple-dyed cloth. She was a believer in God and was among those who had met at a place for prayer. Her heart was opened to Paul's preaching of the gospel, and she and her household became obedient. After she was baptized, she said to them, "If you have judged me to be faithful to the Lord, come to my house and stay" (Acts 16:15, RSV).

Several days later, they were thrown in jail after casting an evil spirit out of a girl who had been following them. They were released from prison miraculously and had the opportunity of preaching the gospel to the jailer. Following his baptism, he took them into his house and set food before them, rejoicing in his obedience to God (Acts 16:16-34).

C. Jesus gives a stern warning that our hospitality is not to be simply an exchange of social graces. If we entertain someone who is expected to return the favor, we have our reward. In inviting the babes in Christ who may be financially or socially unable to entertain us in return, we are obeying the Lord and perhaps saving their souls and ours. Or we may take time to make friends of a neighbor by having her family over for a meal, perhaps while they are moving in and getting their home arranged. In time, because of our hospitality, they may become interested in the Lord, and we or someone else may teach them. It is the gospel which is the power for their salvation, but your hospitality and friendship prepared the heart to receive it. Jesus was so convinced of the importance of hospitality He did much teaching on the subject, saying:

> When you give a luncheon or a dinner, do not invite your friends or your brothers or your relatives or rich neighbors, lest they also invite you in return, and repayment come to you. But when you give a reception, invite the poor, the crippled, the lame, and the blind, and you will be blessed, since they do not have the means to repay you; for you will be repaid at the resurrection of the righteous (Luke 14:12b-14, NASV).

D. Hospitality is a quality of the godly woman. In writing to Timothy, Paul is describing the characteristics to be used when judging a woman's eligibility to be enrolled in special service to the church, thus being given financial support. He wrote, "Let a widow be put on the list only if she is not less than sixty years old, having been the wife of one man, having a reputation for good works; and if she has brought up children, if she has shown hospitality to strangers, if she has washed the saints' feet, if she has assisted those in distress, and if she has devoted herself to every good work" (1 Timothy 5:9,10, NASV). You may recall that, while you may not be 60 years old or applying for support from the church, these attributes may well be goals toward which you work as a younger woman.

    E. An elder must be hospitable (1 Timothy 3:2). Paul precedes his listing of the specific characteristics of an acceptable elder with an imperative "must be." I heard of one elder who said he did not **have** to be hospitable. Paul made no distinction; so if he did not have to be hospitable, neither did he have to be above reproach! The King James says "given to hospitality." In other words, he continues to be hospitable. It is a way of life. Perhaps the requirement that he be the husband of one wife may be partially because she is a vital part in allowing him to be given to hospitality. He surely is genuinely interested in those who need the strength of an elder's hospitality, but it usually is the wife who does the telephoning or visiting to set up the visit, and she does the shopping and prepares a meal which will be both attractive and nutritious. This, in turn, gives the elder the opportunity to provide the spiritual food needed by the weak Christian or a prospect.

    III. During His ministry, Jesus was welcomed into the homes of many of His followers. We are not told whether or not the scribe who offered to follow Jesus wherever He went actually did so. We can imagine that he might have thought it would be an honor to make his home with such a prominent figure. Jesus knew men's thoughts and replied, "The foxes have holes, and the birds of the air have nests; but the Son of man hath not where to lay his head" (Matthew 8:20, KJ).

    A. In Bethany, He stayed at the house of Simon the leper. Jesus must have healed him of that terrible disease; in gratitude, the man who was healed extended his hospitality to his benefactor. It was there that the woman with an alabaster jar of ointment of pure nard anointed His head with the costly preparation (Mark 14:3-9). A similar incident is recorded in Luke 7. A Pharisee invited Jesus to dine with him. While they were reclining at table, a sinful woman of the city (probably Nain) brought an alabaster flask of ointment; standing beside Him, weeping, she wet His feet with her tears, wiped them with her hair, and anointed them with the ointment. Jesus told the Pharisee, who thought to himself that Jesus should have known of the woman's sin, a parable which led him to realize that one who has been forgiven much loves much. Jesus then forgave the woman's sins and told her to go in peace (Luke 7:36-50).

B. All our children know the story of Zacchaeus and the sycamore tree. Jesus surely knew that this man of small stature, so anxious to see Jesus, was a man with a good and honest heart who needed only compassion and teaching. No matter that the man was a hated tax collector. Jesus invited Himself to Zacchaeus' house. The little man scrambled down in a big hurry and received the Lord joyfully. Again, people criticized Jesus for going to stay in the house of a sinner. Zacchaeus, a wealthy man, said he gave half his goods to the poor, and if he had defrauded anyone, he would restore it fourfold. Apparently, in the hearing of the murmuring crowd, Jesus assured him, "Today salvation has come to this house, since he also is a son of Abraham. For the Son of man came to seek and to save the lost" (Luke 19:9,10, RSV).

C. The hospitality of a woman named Martha, who received Jesus into her house, led to a lasting friendship with the son of God. It appears that Martha, Mary, and their brother, Lazarus, were His best personal friends. The story of Mary and Martha has been told and retold to emphasize Jesus' teaching that hearing His teaching was more important than providing Him with physical food (Luke 10:38-42). John tells us that Jesus loved the three, whose home was in Bethany. When Jesus came to their home after Lazarus had died, it was Martha who assured Him that she had believed that He is the Christ, the son of God. Mary joined them on the road with those who had come to comfort them. Many believed in Jesus when He raised His dear friend from death (John 10:1-45).

D. Two men who had heard the women's report that Jesus Christ had arisen and were discussing the events of the past few days were perhaps the most surprised hosts whose story is recorded in the Bible. Jesus joined them as they were walking to Emmaus and asked them what was all this they were talking about. They were surprised that He had not heard, and recounted the whole story to Him. He then began with Moses and the prophets and explained to them the things concerning Himself, the necessity of His suffering and resurrection. They still did not recognize Him, but they urged Him, "Stay with us, for it is getting toward evening, and the day is now nearly over." He accepted, and as they reclined at table, He took the bread and blessed it, broke it, and began giving it to them. We are told that their eyes were opened, they recognized Him, and He vanished from their sight. Then they recalled their feelings while He was expounding the scriptures to them. With joy, they returned to Jerusalem to share their wonderful news (Luke 24:13-33).

Conclusion: Would **you** like to entertain Jesus in your home? You can! Of course, He is with us, in us as our hope of glory. But there is a way that you can actually be a host to **royalty**, the son of God. You can give Him food and drink, clothing, even visit Him in prison. Many times, we have read and discussed the judgment scene which. Jesus described in Matthew 25:31:46. To those on His right, the righteous, the King will say:

> Come, you who are blessed by my Father; take your inheritance, the kingdom prepared for you since the creation of the world. For I was hungry and you gave me something to eat, I was thirsty and you gave me something to drink, I was a stranger and you invited me in, I needed clothes and you clothed me, I was sick and you looked after me, I was in prison and you came to visit me.
>
> Then the righteous will answer him, "Lord, when did we see you hungry and feed you, or thirsty and give you something to drink? When did we see you a stranger and invite you in, or needing clothes and clothe you? When did we see you sick or in prison and go visit you?"
>
> The King will reply, "I tell you the truth, whatever you did for one of the least of these brothers of mine, you did for me" (Matthew 25:34-40, NIV).

What a divine privilege to play host to Jesus Christ, the son of God, as we "contribute to the needs of the saints, practice hospitality"!

Daily Bible Reading

Monday
Our Life and Our Money
(Luke 12:13-34)

Tuesday
Faith and Works
(James 2:14-26)

Wednesday
Help Others to Help Themselves
(2 Thessalonians 3:6-14)

Thursday
Be Hospitable
(1 Peter 4:8-10)

Friday
New Converts Prove Hospitable
(Acts 16:11-34)

Saturday
You Can Do It for Jesus!
(Matthew 25:31-46)

Memory Verses

Luke 6:38

Matthew 25:40

Chapter 12

Rejoice and Weep

Introduction: From sunshine to shadow! Although rejoicing and weeping are at opposite ends of the spectrum of emotions, when we are sharing with others, they spring from a common source—compassion. This is the art of feeling with others. It is showing empathy, actually experiencing their joy or pain.

Our religion must be of both the head and the heart! Jesus said, "God is spirit, and those who worship him must worship in spirit and truth" (John 4:24, RSV). We have been right to emphasize truth, knowing and obeying God's will. In response to those who depend almost wholly on feeling—emotion—in religion, I fear we have, at times, tended to eliminate them from our own Christian worship.

There must be a balance between mind and heart, truth and emotion. Jesus came to do His Father's will; His teaching was that of the Father. He cited God's Word as truth, yet He rejoiced and wept during His ministry.

In this lesson, we are dealing primarily with the emotions of joy and sadness and our reaction to them in others. May our lives present to the world God's truth on these subjects. We have more scripture with which to work than we can cover in one short lesson. We will begin with Paul when he said, "Rejoice with them that do rejoice, and weep with them that weep" (Romans 12:15, KJ).

    I. Our own acts of compassion are reflections of the divine nature demonstrated for us by God and Jesus. Our character becomes more like theirs as we acquire knowledge of them through the scriptures and apply what we learn to spiritual growth.

        A. Ours is a God of compassion. Although we learn of our way to salvation through Christ in the New Testament, we can learn much about God's mercy and justice from the Old Testament. David, who was called a man after God's own heart, knew both the goodness

133

and severity of God. His expressions of repentance, worship, and praise can help us in expressing our own feelings to our Creator. Please read all of Psalm 145; we will quote only a portion here:

Great is the Lord and most worthy of praise;
his greatness no one can fathom.
One generation will commend your works to another;
they will tell of your mighty acts.
They will speak of the glorious splendor of your majesty,
and will meditate on your wonderful works.
They will tell of the power of your awesome works,
and will proclaim your great deeds.
They will celebrate your abundant goodness
and joyfully sing of your righteousness.

The Lord is gracious and compassionate,
slow to anger and rich in love.
The Lord is good to all;
he has compassion on all he has made . . .
The Lord is faithful to all his promises
and loving toward all he has made.
The Lord upholds all those who fall
and lifts up all who are bowed down . . .

The Lord is righteous in all his ways
and loving toward all he has made.
The Lord is near to all who call on him,
to all who call on him in truth.
He fulfills the desires of those who fear him;
he hears their cry and saves them.
The Lord watches over all who love him,
but all the wicked he will destroy.

(Psalm 145:3-9,13b,14,17-20, NIV)

B. During His ministry, Jesus showed compassion to those who were suffering physically and spiritually. He was moved with pity toward the multitudes of bewildered and miserable people who came to hear Him:

And Jesus was going about all the cities and the villages, teaching in their synagogues, and proclaiming the gospel of the kingdom, and healing every kind of disease and every kind of sickness. And seeing the multitudes, he felt compassion for them, because they were distressed and downcast like sheep

134

without a shepherd. Then he said to his disciples, "The harvest is plentiful, but the workers are few. Therefore beseech the Lord of the harvest to send out workers into his harvest" (Matthew 9:35-38, NASV).

Jesus felt sorry for the host of people who were in need of His teaching, as well as for the 5,000 people who had trudged a long way to listen to Him. He realized they must be hungry; in fact, they might faint from fatigue if they were not provided food. He fed them through one of His most spectacular miracles, using a small boy's lunch to feed the throng. He was especially touched by the plea of those who demonstrated faith and humility in their plea for help. One such man was a leper who besought Him, falling on his knees before Him and saying, " 'If you are willing, you can make me clean.' And moved with compassion, he stretched out his hand and touched him, and said to him, 'I am willing; be cleansed' " (Mark 1:40,41, NASV).

II. When we realize the many reasons a Christian has to rejoice, it should not be hard for us to show our compassion by sharing the joy of others. Anyone who might think a long face and doleful speech are true characteristics of the Christian surely has not read her Bible! In preparing this lesson, I was amazed at the many times we find the words **rejoice** and **joy** in the Bible. The two words together fill a good two pages in the fine print of a good concordance. Let's show the joy of salvation by rejoicing!

A. Do we find words of self-pity in Paul's epistles written from prison? No! Over and over, he tells of his own rejoicing, even in suffering, and he tells Christians to rejoice.

His Philippian letter overflows with the words "joy" and "rejoicing." Did he rage when he found that some were preaching Christ out of envy and strife? Certainly not; he knew that others were preaching out of love, and he realized that those preaching from wrong motives still were talking about the Christ. He says, "What then? Only that in every way, whether in pretense or in truth, Christ is proclaimed; and in this I rejoice, yes, and I will rejoice" (Philippians 1:18, NASV).

He urged the Christians to whom he was writing to let their attitudes be those Christ exhibited in coming to the earth to live as a man and to die on the cross. Their remaining faithful would make Paul's suffering worthwhile. He maintained a joyful attitude himself: "But even if I am being poured out as a drink offering upon the sacrifice and service of your faith, I rejoice and share my joy with you all. And you, too, I **urge you**, rejoice in the same way and share your joy with me" (Philippians 2:17,18, NASV).

135

He continues, "Finally, my brethren, rejoice in the Lord" (Philippians 3:1, KJ). As if to emphasize that Christians should express their joy, he repeated, "Rejoice in the Lord always; again I will say, Rejoice" (Philippians 4:4, RSV).

B. To the Thessalonians, Paul indicated that there is to be no end to our overflowing happiness: "Rejoice always, pray constantly, give thanks in all circumstances; for this is the will of God in Christ for you" (1 Thessalonians 5:16-18, RSV).

Rejoice **always**! Paul, did you really mean that we are to rejoice when times are bad? When others put us down? When I am hungry? Through his inspired epistle, we can hear Paul say, "Yes! I did it. But I had help. You can have that same help. You **can** do it!"

I rejoice in the Lord greatly that now at length you have revived your concern for me; you were indeed concerned for me, but you had no opportunity. Not that I complain of want; for I have learned, in whatever state I am, to be content. I know how to be abased, and I know how to abound; in any and all circumstances I have learned the secret of facing plenty and hunger, abundance and want. I can do all things in him who strengthens me (Philippians 4:10-13, RSV).

III. The only time we are not to rejoice is at the misfortune of others, even of our enemies. Although the old law exacted "an eye for an eye and a tooth for a tooth," Jesus showed us a more excellent way to deal with those who mistreat us. However, we learn that righteous Job did not gloat over his enemies' misfortune (Job 31:29,30). Even under the old law, apparently, while the righteous were carrying out the prescribed punishment for the wicked, they were to be sad rather than glad. We hear the wise man saying, "Do not rejoice when your enemy fails, and do not let your heart be glad when he stumbles; lest the Lord see it and be displeased, and he turn away his anger from him" (Proverbs 24:17,18, NASV).

In fact, it appears that one who was glad when calamity befell his enemy would be punished: "He who mocks the poor reproaches his Maker; he who rejoices at calamity will not go unpunished" (Proverbs 17:5, NASV).

The more excellent way Paul mentioned in 1 Corinthians 12:31 is the love he describes so beautifully in Chapter 13. Love teaches us that there are times when we do not rejoice, but it is not because of any suffering or deprivation we experience. Jesus did not curse those who were crucifying Him—He asked God to forgive them. We are not to rejoice in our own unrighteousness or the wicked deeds of others. Agape love loathes the deed itself while grieving and praying for the soul of the sinner. Love "does not rejoice in unrighteousness, but rejoices with the truth" (1 Corinthians 13:6, NASV).

IV. We are to rejoice with those who rejoice. This would seem to be the natural thing to do, but it may depend on our own attitude and our relationship with the one who is rejoicing. Jealousy might enter into the picture. Can you truly be happy for someone who has won a prize for which you were competing, or with someone who just moved to a new, spacious home while you still occupied a cramped house or apartment? Perhaps a neighbor's daughter received an honor you felt your own daughter should have had. Can you rejoice with them and encourage your daughter to do so? At the same time, you can rejoice with your daughter in that she did her best.

A. We join friends and relatives in rejoicing when a child is born. With them, we marvel at the perfection of the tiny infant and at God's wonderful plan for the nurture of so tiny a person by loving parents. If we are good friends, we enjoy seeing the child grow to become a student, and finally we rejoice with them at her graduation. In time, we may be invited to share the festivities connected with her marriage. Our pleasure is greatest when we see her choosing a Christian mate and establishing a Christian home.

B. While all these temporal things are intended to be times of rejoicing, our greatest joy should be in seeing one born into the family of God. Just as a child born into her parent's family is welcomed and loved, so the babe in Christ is to be welcomed and loved by brothers and sisters in the Lord's family. We rejoice with those who have died to sin and are "alive to God in Christ Jesus" (Romans 6:11).

After hearing the gospel from Philip, the Ethiopian eunuch was baptized, then went on his way rejoicing. After the Philippian jailer had heard the word of the Lord from his former prisoners, Paul and Silas, he showed his repentance by washing their wounds; then he and his household were baptized. He took them into his house, set food before them, "and he rejoiced with all his household that he had believed in God" (Acts 16:34, RSV).

C. Just as the members of the physical body are interdependent, so are the members of the Lord's body. Paul says, "For just as the body is one and has many members, and all the members of the body, though many, are one body, so it is with Christ. For by one Spirit we were all baptized into one body—Jews or Greeks, slaves or free— and all were made to drink of one Spirit." He then presents a convincing picture of the human body's functioning because each member performs its own duty, each dependent on the other. He concludes, "If one member suffers, all suffer together; if one member is honored, all rejoice together. Now you are the body of Christ and individually members of it" (1 Corinthians 12:12-26, RSV).

Paul rejoiced that the Roman Christians' obedience was known widely. We rejoice not only in the spiritual growth of Christians in our particular congregation, but we are happy to know of the progress of sister congregations throughout the world. We are happy, too, when it is possible for us to participate, either personally or by financial support, in the Lord's work, giving the glory to God.

D. Through some of His parables, Jesus demonstrated the rejoicing among Christians and even in heaven when a sinner is saved. He was being criticized by the Pharisees because He received and ate with sinners, so He told them this parable:

> What man among you, having a hundred sheep, if he has lost one of them, does not leave the ninety-nine in the wilderness, and go after the one which is lost, until he finds it? And when he has found it, he lays it on his shoulders, rejoicing. And when he comes home, he calls together his friends and his neighbors, saying to them, "Rejoice with me, for I have found my sheep which was lost." Just so, I tell you, there will be more joy in heaven over one sinner who repents than over ninety-nine righteous persons who need no repentance (Luke 15:4-7, RSV).

E. Jesus rejoiced in the progress of His ministry. He sent out the 70, two by two, as forerunners to the towns and places He planned to go. They were to do His work. Those who received them received Him; those who rejected them rejected Jesus, and in so doing rejected God, He told them as He sent them out. We are given no details of their work, only that they returned with joy saying, "Lord, even the demons are subject to us in your name!"

Jesus apparently was pleased with their success, for we read:

> In that same hour he rejoiced in the Holy Spirit and said, "I thank thee, Father, Lord of heaven and earth, that thou hast hidden these things from the wise and understanding and revealed them to babes; yea, Father, for such was thy gracious will. All things have been delivered to me by my Father; and no one knows who the Son is except the Father, or who the Father is except the Son and any one to whom the Son chooses to reveal him" (Luke 10:21,22, RSV).

There may have been a tinge of pride in the 70's report of their power over demons in Jesus' name. He reminded them that He had seen Satan fall from heaven, also that the power they had exercised had come from Him. He wanted them to look toward their final reward saying, "Nevertheless do not rejoice in this, that the spirits are subject to you; but rejoice that your names are written in heaven" (Luke 10:20, RSV).

It is a heavenly privilege to rejoice with fellow Christians here on earth, especially as we join them in rejoicing that **our names** are written in heaven!

V. We must share the sorrow of those who are sad, weep with those who weep. It is a privilege to share the happiness of those about us, but it is also a privilege and a duty to share their tears. In fact, because of our compassion, we will feel their sorrow as keenly as if it were our own. This is an extension of Christian love. After encouraging the Hebrew Christians to continue loving their brothers, the writer counseled, "There are people in jail. Remember them as if you were there too. There are people who are being mistreated. Remember them as though you were suffering with them" (Hebrews 13:3, SEB).

A. One way we can be sure to show compassion to those who are in need of our attention is by associating with fellow Christians in small groups or on a one-to-one basis. One of our brethren has done a survey of a dozen or more congregations and reports that some 50 percent said they did not have a friend with whom they exchanged visits in the congregation where they worship. With all of our modern conveniences, we should have more time to make friends among our fellow Christians and neighbors than our parents or grandparents had. Our conveniences, such as television, may distract us, even occupy too much of our time. Because of our telephones and automobiles, we may become too involved in our own pursuits to have time for others. There may be, within our immediate fellowship, those who are weeping because of failure or disappointment. How can we mingle our tears with theirs if they do not feel close enough to us to let us know their suffering?

B. We may be more inclined to weep with those facing physical illness than with those suffering spiritual illness. Both need our empathy. A member of one congregation commented that we always are careful to announce the names and pray for those ill or in the hospitals, but seldom do we hear a prayer for those who are in need of spiritual guidance. Of course, as Jesus said, we should do the former and not neglect the latter! Quite often, we see Jesus showing compassion for those who were physically afflicted and healing them. Our loving care—doing the things for those who are ill that they are unable to do—may contribute more to their recovery than we think.

Our greatest gift to those facing terminal illness is to help focus their minds on the Christian's hope of a body, to be given by the Lord, which will be subject to no pain or deterioration. This can be accomplished best when we have wept with them through the stages of rejection, anger, bargaining, and finally acceptance. Then we can read with them the beautiful passage from 1 Corinthians 15:35-55, ending with, "Death is swallowed up in victory. O death, where is thy victory? O death, where is thy sting?"

C. The shortest verse in the Bible—"Jesus wept" (John 11:35)—is quoted often as such, but do we realize its full revelation of His compassion? He loved Mary, Martha, and Lazarus. He had been notified of the serious illness Lazarus was experiencing, yet He stayed two days longer in the place where He received the message, saying, "This sickness is not unto death, but for the glory of God, that the Son of God may be glorified by it" (John 11:4, NASV).

When He told His disciples that they would be going to Judea, they protested, for the Jews there had been looking for Him, wanting to stone Him. He told them, "Our friend Lazarus has fallen asleep; but I go, that I may awaken him out of sleep" (John 11:11, NASV).

Jesus told them plainly that Lazarus had died. Thomas may have doubted later, but he said, "Let us also go that we may die with him." He was willing to face the angry Jews with Jesus, even to be stoned with Him.

Both Martha and Mary, upon Jesus' arrival at their home, declared that Lazarus would not have died if Jesus had been there. Martha had gone out to meet Him on the road. She had expressed faith in her brother's resurrection at the judgment and also confessed that she believed Jesus to be the Christ after He told her, "I am the resurrection and the life; he who believes in me shall live even if he dies, and everyone who lives and believes in me shall never die."

The divine side of Jesus knew that He was going to bring Lazarus from the grave, but the human side was deeply moved and visibly distressed when He saw the sisters and those who had come out from Jerusalem to share their sorrow; as they were weeping, Jesus wept.

Some of the mourners commented on Jesus' great love for Lazarus, but some speculated that this One who had opened the eyes of the blind could have kept this one whom He loved so much from dying. Jesus knew that God heard Him always, but He uttered a prayer before calling Lazarus from the tomb and instructing the amazed crowd to unbind him and let him go. We are not told of the great rejoicing of the sisters and their brothers and those who were with them, but we are told that many believed in Jesus because of what they had seen.

We are not told not to weep at the death of Christian friends or loved ones, but we are told not to weep in the same way as those who have no hope. I wept at the bedside of a beloved sister who had been something of a mother figure to me. She had fought a brave but losing battle with cancer. One of the nurses, attempting to console me, said, "You

140

know she is better off." I replied, "Yes, I know. I am not weeping for her, I am weeping for myself, for my loss." She was a faithful Christian; I have every hope of meeting her again at the resurrection. But my path to that reunion will be a little more lonely that it would have been with her here to walk with me. The wonderful thing is that I had the great consolation available to us through Paul's epistle to Christians who were concerned about those who had gone before:

> But we would not have you ignorant, brethren, concerning those who are asleep, that you may not grieve as others do who have no hope. For since we believe that Jesus died and rose again, even so, through Jesus, God will bring with him those who have fallen asleep. For this we declare to you by the word of the Lord, that we who are alive, who are left until the coming of the Lord, shall not precede those who have fallen asleep. For the Lord himself will descend from heaven with a cry of command, with the archangel's call, and with the sound of the trumpet of God. And the dead in Christ will rise first; then we who are alive, who are left, shall be caught up together with them in the clouds to meet the Lord in the air; and so we shall always be with the Lord. Therefore comfort one another with these words (1 Thessalonians 4:13-18, RSV).

D. We may experience the wonderful comfort we receive because of Christian hope while we join Paul in sorrow over those who refuse to accept Christ or, having been born into the body of Christ, have turned back into sin. He rejoiced with those who were rejoicing, yet he wept for those whose eyes were fixed on the earthly rather than the heavenly:

> Join with others in following my example, brothers, and take note of those who live according to the pattern we gave you. For, as I have often told you before and now say again even with tears, many live as enemies of the cross of Christ. Their destiny is destruction, their god is their stomach, and their glory is in their shame. Their mind is on earthly things. But our citizenship is in heaven. And we eagerly await a Savior from there, the Lord Jesus Christ, who, by the power that enables him to bring everything under his control, will transform our lowly bodies so that they will be like his glorious body (Philippians 3:17-21, NIV).

Conclusion: From God's holy Word, we have ample assurance that those who go through life rejoicing over things of the flesh will weep when they face the Lord in judgment:

*You will begin to stand outside and to knock at the door, say-
ing, "Lord, open to us." He will answer you, "I do not know
where you come from." Then you will begin to say, "We ate and
drank in your presence, and you taught in our streets." But he will
say, "I tell you, I do not know where you come from; depart from
me, all you workers of iniquity!" There you will weep and gnash
your teeth (Luke 13:25b-28a, RSV).*

What a glorious privilege it will be for those who have wept with the
troubled and sorrowing when we stand before the Son of Man, to rejoice with those on His right to whom He will say, "Come, you who are
blessed of my Father, inherit the kingdom prepared for you from the
foundation of the world" (Matthew 25:34b, NASV).

Daily Bible Reading

Sunday
God Is Gracious!
(Psalm 145)

Monday
A Compassionate Savior
(Matthew 9)

Tuesday
Rejoice Always!
(Philippians 1, 2, 3, 4)

Wednesday
A More Excellent Way
(1 Corinthians 12:13b, 13:1-13)

Thursday
We Rejoice and Weep Together!
(1 Corinthians 12:4-31)

Friday
Jesus Wept!
(John 11:1-44)

Saturday
Weep Not As Those Who Have No Hope
(1 Thessalonians 4:17-21)

Memory Verses

Philippians 4:4-8

Chapter 13

Our Victory

Introduction: Recognizing the great and wonderful promises given to us through God's gracious love, we present ourselves to Him as a living sacrifice. Realizing that nothing outside ourselves can separate us from the love of Christ, we follow His example toward Christian maturity. We realize that we must prepare ourselves for defense against Satan and his cohorts, but we do this by taking the offensive. We put on the armor of God and, equipped thus, we are ready to heed Paul's admonition, "Be not overcome of evil, but overcome evil with good" (Romans 12:21, KJ).

I. Beware! Don't let evil get the best of you! Jesus was not freed from meeting temptation when He assumed the likeness of man. Satan appealed to Him just as he appeals to us—through the lust of the flesh, the lust of the eye, and the pride of life (Matthew 4:1-11). Peter tells us, "Be of sober spirit, be on the alert, Your adversary, the devil, prowls about like a roaring lion, seeking someone to devour. But resist him, firm in your faith" (1 Peter 5:8,9a, NASV). How can we resist? Just like Jesus did! He used the sword of the Spirit, each time saying, "It is written." Through Christ, we can have full victory, but we must know the enemy we face.

A. We must remember that our enemy is Satan, and that he is able to manifest himself to us in various means of temptation. A family member may invite us to attend some activity which, right in itself, would interfere with our Christian duty. Our young people may be asked to participate in something which would compromise their Christian identity. We who, knowing that our bodies are "temples of the Holy Spirit" and are determined to hold the line against obesity, are tempted easily by an array of beautiful desserts.

1. Jesus minced no words in describing the devil to disbelieving Jews who challenged Him so frequently. In this particular instance, they first were incensed when He told them the truth would make them free. They prided themselves on the fact that they were descendants of Abraham and were enslaved to no one. The Master Teacher then pointed out that everyone who commits sin is a slave to sin. Again, they affirmed that Abraham was their father. Jesus told them bluntly that they would do what Abraham did if they were His children. They then protested that they were children of God. Jesus replied:

> *If God were really your Father, then you would love me. I came from God and now I am here. I did not come by my own authority. God sent me. You don't understand these things I say. Why? It is because you cannot accept my teaching. Your father is the devil. You belong to him. You want to do what he wants. The devil was a murderer from the beginning. The devil was against the truth. And there is no truth in the devil. He is like the lies he tells. The devil is a liar, and he is the father of lies. I speak the truth. That is why you don't believe me (John 8:42-45, ERV).*

Beware! The devil is a murderer, is against the truth, and is himself a liar and the father of lies!

2. Satan worked through a magician at the beginning of Paul's first missionary journey. He, Barnabas, and John Mark had worked their way through the Island of Cyprus to Paphos. Sergius Paulus, a government official, was described as an intelligent man. He called the missionaries to him and asked to hear the word of God. Elymas, the magician, opposed them and tried to turn the governor away from them. Paul, filled with the Holy Spirit, looked him right in the eye and made it quite plain that the man was serving the devil:

> *"You son of the devil, you enemy of all righteousness, full of all deceit and villainy, will you not stop making crooked the straight paths of the Lord? And now, behold, the hand of the Lord is upon you, and you shall be blind and unable to see the sun for a time." Immediately mist and darkness fell upon him and he went about seeking people to lead him by the hand. Then the proconsul believed, when he saw what had occurred, for he was astonished at the teaching of the Lord (Acts 13:10-12, RSV).*

Magic! We are all intrigued by the tricks of magicians. Now, we are not talking about our friends who entertain us with parlor tricks, but we do need to be wary of the occult. A friend who grew up with our younger daughter was showing us all kinds of things, which he performed so quickly that we simply could not understand how he was able to fool us so completely.

I wanted to know how he did it, so I asked, "John, how do you make us see a scarf turn into a rabbit? We know there is some trick to it. How do you do it?"

"Very carefully!" was his smiling reply.

We need to be just as careful not to be fooled by the "sons of the devil" who pervert the truth of God. We may be most easily deceived by that which is closest to the truth. Therefore, we must be careful to know the truth, and the truth will keep us free from following error. In the above scripture, Satan's tool was described as the enemy of all that is right, full of evil tricks and lies—even trying to change the Lord's truths into lies. Beware!

B. In his epistles, Paul warned that the devil, through his agents, was busily opposing the early Christians. He reminded them that they were spiritually dead when they drifted along on the stream of worldly ideas and obeyed the world's unseen ruler at work in those who were disobedient. Those who attempt to justify doing what comes naturally should pay close attention to this scripture:

> And you he made alive, when you were dead through the trespasses and sins in which you once walked, following the course of this world, following the prince of the power of the air, the spirit that is now at work in the sons of disobedience. Among these we all once lived in the passions of our flesh, following the desires of body and mind, and so we were by nature children of wrath, like the rest of mankind (Ephesians 2:1-3, RSV).

C. Just as darkness is opposed to light, the devil can't stand to be near God. So the way to escape Satan's temptations is to stay close to God! We are promised that God will provide a way to escape temptation; the way will be provided, but we must do the escaping: "The only temptations that you have are the same temptations that all people have. But you can trust God. He will not let you be tempted more than you can bear. But when you are tempted, God will also give you a way to escape that temptation. Then you will be able to endure it" (1 Corinthians 10:13, ERV).

We can't afford to flirt with the world and, thereby, become the enemy of God. We become His friend, able to walk close to God, by keeping the commandments of Jesus. By putting ourselves in the Lord's hands, we can be sure the devil will leave us alone:

> God will give you strength to overcome. That is why the scripture says, "God is against those who are proud, but he gives help to humble people" (Proverbs 3:34).

So, put yourselves under God's authority. Resist the devil and he will run away from you. Get close to God and God will get close to you. Wash your hands of sin, you sinners. Make your hearts pure, you who have divided hearts. Be sad, be sorry, and cry. Change your laughter into crying. Turn your joy into sadness. Be humble before the Lord and he will lift you up (James 4:6-10, SEB).

II. The world says, "If you do me dirty, I'll get even with you!" No! No! Paul says, "Recompense to no man evil for evil" (Romans 12:17a, KJ). Jesus, in the sermon on the mount, gave us what we call "The Golden Rule": "Therefore all things whatsoever ye would that men should do to you, do ye even so to them: for this is the law and the prophets" (Matthew 7:12, KJ).

When I was teaching a junior high school girls' class, one of the girls said, "That means that I can do to anyone else what he does to me!"

After I had explained to her that she had missed the true meaning—that she is to treat others as she wants them to treat her—she replied, "Well, I like it better the way I said it." How true to the world's view!

A. The attitude of retaliation was forbidden even before Jesus came to teach us Christian principles. The wise man of old said, "Do not say, 'I'll do to him as he has done to me; I'll pay that man back for what he did' " (Proverbs 24:29, NIV).

B. We invariably get into trouble when we try to take over God's business. Ishmael was born when Abraham, at Sarah's suggestion, took Hagar as a concubine. It had become hard for them to believe that God would, in His good time, give them the son of promise, through whom the whole world would be blessed. Trouble began even before Ishmael was born, and it continues even today between the descendants of Ishmael and Isaac. Just as surely, we will be in trouble if we take vengeance into our own hands. Paul wrote, "My friends, don't try to punish people when they do wrong to you. Wait for God to punish them with his anger. It is written, 'I am the one who punishes; I will pay people back,' says the Lord" (Romans 12:19, ERV).

III. Our next step, after leaving vengeance for wrongs done to us to God, is actually to bless those who persecute us. Paul says, "Bless them which persecute you: bless, and curse not" (Romans 12:14, KJ). We are told that the Greek word translated **bless** in this instance means "to invoke blessings upon a person." Take the offender to God in prayer!

Rather than praying "God, he did me wrong. Please pay him back for me," we will, if we want to be like Christ, pray, "Father, forgive him, for he did not know what he was doing. Please help him to realize his error and make his life right with you. Then I can fellowship him as a brother."

Much publicity has been given to a trial in which a woman is suing an eldership who withdrew fellowship from her. The elders have said that they had pleaded with her to repent of a sin which was bringing reproach on the church, and that they announced withdrawal of fellowship sorrowfully in the hope that she would be brought back to the Lord. A number of times, we heard prayers led in the church, asking God to bless the elders thus involved, and of course it was right for us to join in those prayers. Finally, though, a young woman suggested to a ladies' group that we pray, also, for the young woman. Surely, the elders of the congregation have continued to pray for her restoration. We needed just to be reminded to join them in praying for her soul!

A. James calls our attention forcefully to the mistakes we can make with our tongues. He says that a person who makes no such mistakes is perfect, and of course we know that Jesus Christ is the only one who was perfect as He lived on earth. The writer describes the tongue as an unruly evil, full of deadly poison. He continues:

With it we bless the Lord and Father, and with it we curse men, who are made in the likeness of God. From the same mouth come blessing and cursing. My brethren, this ought not to be so (James 3:9,10, RSV).

B. Have you ever said something bad about a person, hoping that she never would hear what you said? Then, were you surprised when she gave you a cold shoulder, refusing to speak to you? Perhaps you wished, after you made the snide remark, that you had not said it. An old story tells of a person who thus repented of something she had said. She went to a wise man and asked what she could do. He told her to take a feather pillow and empty its contents into the wind. She did so. He then told her to go pick up every one of the feathers. Of course, the wind had carried them far away, and the task he assigned her was impossible. His wise observance was, "It is so with words we speak!"

Solomon put it this way: "Furthermore, in your bedchamber do not curse a king, and in your sleeping rooms do not curse a rich man, for a bird of the heavens will carry the sound, and the winged creature will make the matter known" (Ecclesiastes 10:20, NASV). Maybe that's the origin of the saying "A little bird told me!"

IV. In order to be victorious over evil, we must overcome it with good. If we are to take the offensive in the battle, we are to be prepared. Paul describes the full armor of God:

Stand firm then, with the belt of truth buckled around your waist, with the breastplate of righteousness in place, and with your

149

*feet fitted with the readiness that comes from the gospel of peace.
In addition to all this, take up the shield of faith, with which you
can extinguish all the flaming arrows of the evil one. Take the
helmet of salvation and the sword of the Spirit, which is the word
of God. And pray in the Spirit on all occasions with all kinds of
prayers and requests (Ephesians 6:14-18, NIV).*

Unlike carnal warfare, we will be using our armor to do good for our
enemy. We will do our best to let him see the truth working in our lives
and, if at all possible, we will share the truth with him. We will pray that
he will be blessed with the righteousness which we practice as we pursue
the gospel of peace. Our faith may even shield our former enemy from
the temptation Satan hurls at us. Blessed and protected in our salvation,
we will turn to the word of God with which, as our sword, we are able to
overcome false doctrine.

A. By providing physical needs of our enemies, we are told
in the scripture that their attitudes can be changed. Then they may be
converted and become not only our friend, but a brother or sister in
Christ. It has been rather popular, especially in the 1960s and 1970s, to
criticize the American government. However, the action of our government and individual Americans in helping to succor and heal our
enemies once they have surrendered is a measure of greatness. It could
be the reason we have been blessed. We helped rebuild Japan, and
have seen her become a powerful industrial nation. We have been a
friend to Italy, and have helped our allies recover from the effects of the
war. Men who served in the armed forces helped in caring for orphans
and in providing food and clothing to those in need. Then they went
back, with the help of brethren at home, and established churches to
supply the spiritual needs of their former enemies. God's plan for overcoming evil with good does work if we will only work it.

B. Paul quoted from Proverbs 25:21,22 when he wrote, "If
your enemy is hungry, feed him. If he is thirsty, give him something to
drink. By doing this, you will make him burn up with shame" (Romans
12:20, SEB). We are more familiar with other translations which
say, "By so doing you will heap burning coals upon his head" (RSV).
That always had a tinge of vengeance to me. But we realize that, at least
as Paul was applying it, the burning shame might well lead to godly sorrow which, in turn, would lead to repentance.

C. You have heard, I'm sure, the saying "Like father, like
son." When we become Christians, we call God our heavenly Father.
We must go beyond, then, the pity which might prompt us to furnish
physical needs to our enemies. We must love our enemies. Someone
has said that there is a valid difference between the love we have for our

families and close friends, as well as the fervent love we are to have for brothers and sisters in Christ, and that shown our enemies. We may not feel the affection we share with our loved ones, but we certainly are to have the **agape**—the love which is concerned with their welfare. We may hate their deeds, but we are interested in their souls. We love them. This is a part of Jesus' teaching in the sermon on the mount, as recorded in both Matthew and Luke:

> You have heard that this was said: "Love your friend and hate your enemy." But I say this to you: Love your enemies! Pray for those who are cruel to you, so that you will become sons of your Father, who is in heaven. God's sun shines upon good people and bad people. It rains upon the people who do right and upon those who do wrong. If you love only those people who love you, then you are not any better than anyone else. Even tax collectors do the same thing! If you greet only your brothers, what more are you doing? Even people without God do the same thing! You must be mature, as your Father in heaven is (Matthew 5:43-48, SEB).

Love and prayer for our enemies can work wonders in our lives as well as in theirs; it is hard to hate someone for whom you are praying. It is just as hard to curse or fight someone you love. You will grow spiritually as you develop the capacity to love and pray for someone who has wronged you. You will be walking toward maturity and perfection. You will be more like your Father.

V. When we have overcome evil with good, a great victory is ours, yet with Paul we say, "It is not I who live; Christ lives in me." God is for us; no person can defeat us. Jesus died for us and has risen again to sit at God's right hand, interceding for us. We feel secure in Christ's love:

> Who shall separate us from the love of Christ? Shall trouble or hardship or persecution or famine or nakedness or danger or sword? . . . No, in all these things we are more than conquerors through him who loved us. For I am convinced that neither death nor life, neither angels nor demons, neither the present nor the future, nor any powers, neither height nor depth, nor anything else in all creation, will be able to separate us from the love of God that is in Christ Jesus our Lord (Romans 8:35,37-39, NIV).

    A. Our obedient faith in Christ Jesus has given us this victory. Because God loved us enough to give us His son, we love Him. We want to please God because of our love for Him. John wrote to Christians:

Loving God means obeying his commands. And God's com-
mands are not too hard for us. Why? Because every person that is
a child of God has the power to win against the world. It is our
faith that has won the victory against the world. So who is the per-
son that wins against the world? Only the person who believes
that Jesus is the Son of God (1 John 5:3-5, ERV).

   B. To the victor belong the spoils. The joys awaiting you in heaven are unspeakably greater than any earthly victory could possibly give. Earthly gain will be only temporary. Heavenly rewards are forever. Awaiting us in heaven with God and Jesus are the patriarchs of old and saints of all ages, many of whom we have loved on earth. With them, we will enjoy the holy city, the new Jerusalem. "God will wipe away every tear from their eyes. There will be no more death, sadness, crying, or pain" (Revelation 21:4, ERV).
   While the victorious are claiming their eternal inheritance in glory, those who have rejected the Father and Son on earth will receive their reward in torment:

The one on the throne said to me, "It is finished! I am the Alpha
and the Omega, the beginning and the end. I will give free water
from the spring of the water of life to any person who is thirsty.
Any person who wins the victory will receive all this. And I will be
his God and he will be my son. But the people who are cowards,
people who refuse to believe, people who do terrible things,
people who kill, people who sin sexually, people who do evil
magic, people who worship idols, and people who tell lies — all
those people will have a place in the lake of burning sulfur. This is
the second death (Revelation 21:6-8, ERV).

   For the victorious, everything in the holy city will be new and beautiful. No earthly words can do justice to its splendor. The new person, having received a body pleasing to God, will be clothed, nourished, and blessed by the Creator of the world.
   1. They will wear clothes by the greatest designer! About those in Sardis who had not soiled their clothes, John was told to write, "They will walk with me, dressed in white, for they are worthy. He who overcomes will, like them, be dressed in white. I will never erase his name from the book of life, but will acknowledge his name before my Father and his angels" (Revelation 3:4b,5, NIV).
   2. They will have access to the fruit forbidden to Adam and Eve after they had sinned: "To him who overcomes, I will give the right to eat from the tree of life, which is in the paradise of God" (Revelation 2:7b, NIV).

3. They will occupy a position of honor among the most glorious assembly ever to be known. Our greatest longing as Christians has been to be near to God and Christ. We are promised, "To him who is victorious I will grant a place on my throne, as I myself was victorious and sat down with my Father on his throne" (Revelation 3:21, NEB).

Conclusion: Those of us privileged to hear the summons "Come, O blessed of my Father, inherit the kingdom prepared for you from the foundation of the world" truly will be **more than conquerors**! Through God's power working in us, with Christ as our mediator, and with the pleadings for us of the Holy Spirit, we will have overcome the world.

Daily Bible Reading

Sunday
Victory Over Temptation
(Matthew 4:1-11)

Monday
Jesus Talks With "Children of the Devil"
(John 8:12-58)

Tuesday
From Death to Life
(Ephesians 2:1-22)

Wednesday
Get Close to God!
(James 4:1-10)

Thursday
A Living Sacrifice
(Romans 12:1-11)

Friday
Put On God's Armor
(Ephesians 6:10-18)

Saturday
More Than Conquerors
(Romans 8:1-39)

Memory Verses

1 John 5:3-5

Epilogue

Let's now turn back to the 12th chapter of Romans and hear again Paul's admonition outlining practical Christianity:

> *I urge you therefore, brethren, by the mercies of God, to present your bodies a living and holy sacrifice, acceptable to God, which is your spiritual service of worship. And do not be conformed to this world, but be transformed by the renewing of your mind, that you may prove what the will of God is, that which is good and acceptable and perfect . . . I say to every man among you not to think more highly of himself than he ought to think; but to think so as to have sound judgment, as God has allotted to each a measure of faith. For just as we have many members in one body and all the members do not have the same function, so we, who are many, are one body in Christ, and individually members one of another . . . Let love be without hypocrisy . . . not lagging in diligence, fervent in spirit, serving the Lord; rejoicing in hope, persevering in tribulation, devoted to prayer, contributing to the needs of the saints, practicing hospitality. Bless those who persecute you; bless and curse not. Rejoice with those who rejoice, and weep with those who weep . . . Do not be overcome by evil, but overcome evil with good (Romans 12:1,2,3b-5,9a, 11-15,21, NASV).*

My prayer is that your sacrificial life will be filled with such joy and radiance that others will walk with you toward the New Jerusalem, where you will have the right to the tree of life and will partake of the water of life freely.

Bibliography

Cruden's Complete Concordance, edited by A. D. Adams, C. H. Irwin, S. A. Waters, C.E.I. Publishing Co., Box 858, Athens, Alabama, 1949.

An Expository Dictionary of New Testament Words, W. E. Vine, Fleming H. Revell Company, Old Tappan, New Jersey, 1940.

Holy Bible, New International Version, Zondervan Bible Publishers, Grand Rapids, Michigan, 1978, revision, 1983 (NIV).

New American Standard Bible, Regal Books, a division of Gospel Light Publications, Glendale, California, U.S.A. (NASV).

The Bible, Revised Standard Version, American Bible Society, New York, 1970 (RSV).

The Holy Bible, American Standard Version, Thomas Nelson & Sons, New York, 1901 (ASV).

The New Testament in Four Versions, King James, Revised Standard, Phillips, New English Bible, The Iverson Ford Associates, New York, New York, 1963 (KJ, RSV, P, NEB).

The New Testament, A New Easy-to-Read Version, Baker Book House, Grand Rapids, Michigan, 1978 (ERV).

The Simple English Bible, International Bible Foundation, Dallas, Texas, 1981 (SEB).

The New Chain Reference Bible, containing Thompson's Chain Reference and Text Cyclopedia, Frank Charles Thompson, D.D., Ph.D., B. B. Kirkbride Bible Co., Indianapolis, Indiana, U.S.A., 1929.

Webster's New Collegiate Dictionary, G. & C. Merriam Co., Springfield, Massachusetts, U.S.A., 1953.